S0-BDQ-482

# Shakespeare's Style

# Shakespeare's Style

## Maurice Charney

FAIRLEIGH DICKINSON UNIVERSITY PRESS
Madison • Teaneck

Published by Fairleigh Dickinson University Press
Copublished by The Rowman & Littlefield Publishing Group, Inc.
4501 Forbes Boulevard, Suite 200, Lanham, Maryland 20706
www.rowman.com

16 Carlisle Street, London W1D 3BT, United Kingdom

Copyright © 2014 by Maurice Charney

*All rights reserved.* No part of this book may be reproduced in any form or by any
electronic or mechanical means, including information storage and retrieval systems,
without written permission from the publisher, except by a reviewer who may quote
passages in a review.

British Library Cataloguing in Publication Information Available

**Library of Congress Cataloging-in-Publication Data**

Charney, Maurice.
Shakespeare's style / Maurice Charney.
pages cm
Includes bibliographical references and index.
ISBN 978-1-61147-764-1 (cloth : alk. paper) -- ISBN 978-1-61147-765-8 (electronic)
1. Shakespeare, William, 1564-1616--Literary style. I. Title.
PR3072.C44 2014
822.3'3--dc23

2014025021

∞™ The paper used in this publication meets the minimum requirements of American
National Standard for Information Sciences Permanence of Paper for Printed Library
Materials, ANSI/NISO Z39.48-1992.

Printed in the United States of America

For

Bobbie

Muse of Divagations

# Contents

# Acknowledgments

Shakespeare's plays are quoted from *The Complete Signet Classic Shakespeare*, ed. Sylvan Barnet (New York: Harcourt Brace Jovanovich, 1972), with the exception of *King Lear*, which is quoted from the Arden edition, 3rd series, ed. R. A. Foakes (London: Thomson Learning, 1997). I follow the chronological order of the plays as listed in the Signet edition. I have profited greatly from the notes in the Signet and Arden editions, from my wide reading in the critical literature about Shakespeare, and from stimulating conversations with my students, academic colleagues, and the members of the Shakespeare Seminar at Columbia University.

# Introduction

*Shakespeare's Style* offers a close reading of all of Shakespeare's plays, with each short chapter devoted to a single aspect of Shakespeare's art. I use the word "style" in a wide sense that includes how characters are fashioned, what key words and images are used to express a play's distinctive meanings, as well as the important nonverbal, presentational aspect of the plays as seen or imagined in performance. Although not strictly a scholarly book (it has no footnotes or bibliography), *Shakespeare's Style* is nevertheless aimed at committed readers and spectators of Shakespeare's plays and the growing number of Shakespeare's plays that may be seen in movies or on television. The book grows out of the same effort to understand the complexity of the vast critical inquiry about Shakespeare's art as the scholarly books I have written.

These include *Shakespeare's Roman Plays: The Function of Imagery in the Drama* (1961), dealing with verbal and nonverbal aspects of *Julius Caesar, Antony and Cleopatra*, and *Coriolanus; Style in "Hamlet"* (1969); *Hamlet's Fictions* (1988, reissued 2014); *Titus Andronicus* (1990); *Shakespeare on Love and Lust* (2000); *Wrinkled Deep in Time: Aging in Shakespeare* (2009); and *Shakespeare's Villains* (2012). But with serious students of Shakespeare also in mind, I have written a different kind of book in *How to Read Shakespeare* (1971, revised 1992) and *All of Shakespeare* (1993). The latter deals comprehensively with all of Shakespeare's works. *Shakespeare's Style* is a kind of sequel to *All of Shakespeare*, except that it is directed to Shakespeare's plays alone, and it concerns itself with only a single aspect of style in each play.

I do not use the idea of Shakespeare's style in its narrower, rhetorical sense, referring only to effects of language. The Roman writer Quintilian of the first century CE established elaborate rhetorical categories for Latin that were taken over by English theorists such as George Puttenham in his *Art of English Poesy* (1589). One frequently used rhetorical device in Shakespeare is "zeugma," which the *Oxford English Dictionary* (OED) defines as "A figure by which a single word is made to refer to two or more words in the sentence." Another frequent rhetorical figure in Shakespeare is "hendiadys," which the OED defines as "A figure of speech in which a single complex idea is expressed by two words connected by a conjunction." A variety of "hendiadys" is in the compacted phrase "sleepy bed," meaning bed in which I am asleep. One can pursue this subject in detail in the excellent study by Sister Miriam Joseph, *Shakespeare's Use of the Arts of Language* (1947).

I am also interested in how characters are conceived and fashioned. I do not mean to practice old-fashioned character analysis, but it is significant how characters are created stylistically. "Old-fashioned" Shakespeare criticism usually refers to romantic and often sentimental writers on Shakespeare of the nineteenth century. I am thinking, particularly, of Sir Sidney Lee's biography, *A Life of William Shakespeare* (1898), in which Prospero in *The Tempest* is seen as an autobiographical portrait of Shakespeare himself bidding farewell to the stage and retiring as a dramatist. This cannot be factually true, and Lee's thinking violates the fictionality of Shakespeare's characters. There is no consistent line of development in these characters. His representations of women, for example, vary widely from the vivacious and intelligent females of the comedies, like Rosalind in *As You Like It* and Beatrice in *Much Ado About Nothing*, to the relatively passive and long-suffering women of the tragedies, like Ophelia in *Hamlet* and Desdemona in *Othello*.

Shakespeare's plays are not directly autobiographical. One of the most curious examples of the way that Shakespeare's "mythical sorrows" enter into Shakespeare criticism is in H. Somerville's *Madness in Shakespearian Tragedy* (1929), which claims that Shakespeare himself was suffering from the brain damage brought about by syphilis when he created the character of Timon in *Timon of Athens*.

We need to insist on the fictionality of Shakespeare's characters. This is where stylistic considerations play an important part. Hamlet is one of the most well-rounded and fully developed characters in all of Shakespeare, but there are seeming contradictions in his presentation on stage. If he is a character who thinks too much (and that is the root of his tragedy, as in the movie with Laurence Olivier), he is also quite homicidal in his pursuit of revenge. In act 3, scene 3, he doesn't consider it a good revenge to kill the king while he is praying, and, in the next scene, he runs Polonius through without ascertaining whether or not his victim is indeed the king. If Hamlet's tragedy is really caused by the fact that he thinks too much, how does one explain his soliloquy at the end of act 3, scene 2, where he says: "Now could I drink hot blood / And do such bitter business as the day / Would quake to look on" (3.2.398–400). He is steeling himself not to murder his mother. Shakespeare seems to be arranging various aspects of Hamlet's character for their maximum theatrical effect.

I am particularly concerned with the plays as they are performed, which would include nonverbal, presentational imagery, although I understand that most people are acquainted with Shakespeare primarily through reading. We must allow for effects in Shakespeare's plays that are nonverbal, that are presented in the dramatic action without the need for an accompanying verbal description. I am thinking of the climactic scene in *Coriolanus* (5.3), when the protagonist is most intent on taking his revenge on the Rome that has exiled him. After many fruitless appeals from his dear friends and family to relent, he answers the fervent oration of his mother with a wordless stage direction: "*Holds her by the hand, silent*" (5.3.182 s.d.). Nothing else need be said, but Coriolanus knows that his gracious pardon will prove "most mortal to him" (5.3.189).

We need to understand that Shakespeare's magnificent language is only one part of the entire dramatic context—and, in any case, the words are spoken by actors on the stage, and different actors will, undoubtedly, speak the words differently. Let us look at one other example (although there are many hundreds to choose from): *Antony and Cleopatra* begins with a speech by Philo, one of Antony's soldiers (who has no other function in the play). He condemns his general's "dotage" (1.1.1), or foolishness, especially connected with elderly lovers, for being so enamored of Cleopatra. "His captain's heart" (1.1.6) "is become the bellows and the fan / To cool a gypsy's lust" (1.1.9–10). "Gypsy" was an Elizabethan word for Egyptian. Philo's speech is interrupted by an elaborate stage direction: "*Flourish. Enter Antony, Cleopatra, her Ladies, the Train, with Eunuchs fanning her*" (1.1.9 s.d.). The stage direction enacts what Philo is saying, and when he continues his speech, he comments on what the audience has clearly seen for itself:

> Look where they come:
> Take but good note, and you shall see in him
> The triple pillar of the world transformed
> Into a strumpet's fool. Behold and see. (1.1.10–13)

The idea of presentational imagery is that it vividly shows the audience what is also spoken about in the language of the play. When Antony is decisively defeated by Caesar at the battle of Actium, all his grief seems to be embodied in the stage direction: "*Sits down*" (3.11.24 s.d.). What more need be said?

I recognize the importance of ideas and backgrounds in Shakespeare, but these are not my primary concern. In *Antony and Cleopatra*, for example, we cannot escape the continuous concern for the conflict between Rome and Egypt, for Antony's conflicted roles as Roman soldier and Egyptian lover. These are ideas drawn from Sir Thomas North's translation of Plutarch's

*Lives*, which Shakespeare made significant and often literal use of. But I use the conflict of Rome and Egypt not historically but stylistically: in other words, how Antony's overarching historical moment is expressed in the imagery of the play. I don't intend to ignore the big ideas that the plays are about, but my focus is on how they are expressed. *Macbeth* is a play deeply steeped in Scottish history as Shakespeare read about it in Raphael Holinshed's *Chronicles* (1577) and other historical sources, but my primary concern is not with how Shakespeare interpreted Scottish history but with his imaginative creation of tragic characters who enact this history. Influenced by his reading of Holinshed's *Chronicles*, Shakespeare devoted at least ten plays to English history: the Minor Tetralogy (*Richard III* and the three parts of *Henry VI*), the Major Tetralogy (*Richard II*, the two parts of *Henry IV*, and *Henry V*), *King John*, and *Henry VIII*, but, while the history behind the plays is fascinating in its own right, my concern is with the expression of dramatic values rather than with the plays' status as histories.

But such matters are not my chief concern, which is with a close reading of the text itself. I am particularly interested in discovering the preoccupations of the dramatist, both verbal and nonverbal. In *Hamlet*, for example, there are a significant number of skin images, especially related to disease. When Hamlet meets Fortinbras's Captain in act 4, scene 4, he complains about the folly of his military expedition:

> Two thousand souls and twenty thousand ducats
> Will not debate the question of this straw.
> This is th' imposthume of much wealth and peace,
> That inward breaks, and shows no cause without
> Why the man dies. (4.4.25–29)

An "imposthume" is a boil or abscess, and it calls our attention to the poisoned secrecy of the play and its many murderous plots. Shakespeare's imagery has been much studied since Caroline Spurgeon's important book, *Shakespeare's Imagery and What It Tells Us* (1936), followed by Wolfgang Clemen's *The Development of Shakespeare's Imagery* (1951, first published in 1936 in German). Most of Shakespeare's plays have a distinctive set of key images, both in the language and in the staging. The repeated use of these images in any particular play offers useful clues for the interpretation of that play.

Close reading may also be pursued in key words that are not necessarily images. I am thinking of the use of "ha" in *Othello*. This is an insignificant word, usually called a meaningless interjection, but it has special significance in the context of this play. It is characteristically Iago's word, which, as Cassio is leaving Desdemona, he uses to initiate Othello's jealousy. With some annoyance, Iago exclaims: "Ha! I like not that" (3.3.35). This provokes

Othello into a series of questions about his wife's conduct. More importantly, it is interesting to see how Othello takes up Iago's word later in the scene (3.3.330) and how it signifies Iago's successful seduction of Othello.

Following is a preview of the thirty-four short chapters of this book.

We begin with *The Comedy of Errors* and Antipholus of Syracuse as an ideal comic hero. He is searching for his lost twin brother in Ephesus, but, when he is mistaken for that brother, he does nothing significant to assert his own identity. In true comic style, he entertains "the offered fallacy" even though he knows it to be wrong. He decides to accept the many gifts and favors that are showered upon him.

*Love's Labor's Lost*, modeled on John Lyly, does a good deal to satirize learning, especially with such extreme characters as Holofernes the school-master, Nathaniel the curate, and Don Armado the "fantastical Spaniard." They are all at ease in their preoccupation with words, especially words derived from Latin. It is as if the rapidly developing English language has been set back a hundred years.

The physical deformities of Richard, Duke of Gloucester, later King Richard III, figure importantly in the action of the third part of *Henry VI* and *Richard III*. Richard seems uniquely satisfied with his ugliness, which allows him scope for his self-confessed villainy. He is astonished at his own success, even in the wooing of Anne for his queen.

Aaron in *Titus Andronicus* sets the pattern for many of Shakespeare's villains that follow, like Iago in *Othello*. He begins the play in Marlovian splendor, even though he is a captive to Titus. He is a sardonic, laughing villain, who reminds us of the medieval Vice. Tamora, the Queen of the Goths—also a captive—is his devoted mistress. Unlike other villains like Iago, Aaron has one redeeming trait: his absolute love for his black baby, conceived with Tamora.

*The Taming of the Shrew* is a paradoxical play because it is ultimately difficult to tell who tames whom. Petruchio seems to have the upper hand in socializing Kate, as one would train a hawk, but, eventually, Kate becomes aware of how the marriage game is played and seems to triumph at the end. At the conclusion, Petruchio and Kate win a large bet and look like a happily married couple.

The conventions of romantic love are formally displayed in *The Two Gentlemen of Verona*. Valentine's contempt for love at the beginning of the play is strongly rejected in act 2, when he falls desperately in love with Silvia. Soon Proteus is falling in love with Silvia, too, and he decisively rejects his former love for Julia. The swiftness of all of these moves looks forward to the chemically induced loves of *A Midsummer Night's Dream*. It is significant that the women in *The Two Gentlemen of Verona* seem much more convincing lovers than the men.

*Romeo and Juliet* begins as a comedy, but the feud between the Capulets and the Montagues turns deadly with the death of Mercutio. Tybalt, the swordsman, seems to be at the heart of the tragedy, which unfolds with great emphasis on portents and inauspicious stars. There is a sense of doom that hangs over the play.

In *Richard II*, it is remarkable how our attitudes to Richard change during the course of the play. In the earlier scenes, the frivolous Richard insults the dying Gaunt and seizes his estate, which properly belongs to Gaunt's son, Henry. Richard alienates the audience when he unjustly "farms" the realm to pay for his Irish wars. But when he returns from Ireland, he hardly fights Bolingbroke at all, all the while asserting the divine right of kings. At the time of his murder in Pomfret Castle, he has become a Christ-like martyr in his sufferings.

It is important to remember that the fairies in *A Midsummer Night's Dream* are not mortals but spirits, who are amoral and not in any way Christian. Titania, Queen of the Fairies, is uninhibited in her love for Bottom, the weaver, even though Oberon, King of the Fairies, has turned him into an ass. Puck, Oberon's factotum, is Robin Goodfellow, a mischievous spirit who enacts Oberon's orders to induce love chemically with the juice of a magical pansy.

Shylock seems hardly a comic character in *The Merchant of Venice*. His monomaniacal hatred of Antonio and his insistence on the pound of flesh when Antonio doesn't pay his bond all seem like the dire events of tragedy. Shylock rationalizes his desire for revenge by the hateful way that Jews have been treated in Venice. The flight of his daughter, Jessica, who marries a Christian and steals from her father, further enrages him, and he asks unequivocally: "Hates any man the thing he would not kill?"

In *King John*, "commodity" is a key word, much used by Philip Faulconbridge, the bastard son of Richard, *Coeur de lion*. The Bastard seems to take over the play from King John. His reaction to the deal between the English and French kings—to leave off warring because of the proposed marriage between Lewis, the Dauphin of France, and Blanch of Spain, niece to King John—invokes the base idea of commodity, which has a range of meanings: self-interest, gain, expediency, commercial advantage, and profit. This is the way of the world, which the Bastard vigorously rejects.

Falstaff in the two parts of *Henry IV* is a creative and imaginative speaker and an excellent actor. He is particularly skilled in hyperbole, or what we would ordinarily call exaggeration, or just plain lying. His speeches are self-conscious thrustings beyond the ordinary and commonplace. The fact that he is a fat man gives a literal meaning to his hyperbole. He is a gormandizer with an unquenchable appetite for food and drink.

Falstaff's banishment at the end of *2 Henry IV* is a significant event. Prince Hal, now King Henry V, does what he has always hinted he would do, and the rejection of his boon companion of the tavern in Eastcheap is predictable. Yet it comes with a harsh cruelty: "I know thee not old man" (5.5.47). Falstaff has always insisted on his everlasting youth. He dies shortly thereafter in *Henry V*.

The chapter on Shakespeare's illiterates is somewhat speculative, but Dame Quickly (in the *Henry IV* plays and in *The Merry Wives of Windsor*) and the Nurse in *Romeo and Juliet* speak as if they know the language only phonetically. Their many malapropisms and spoonerisms come naturally to characters who don't know how to read or write. Princess Katherine in *Henry V* is clearly not illiterate, but her English lesson is also entirely phonetic, and she discovers that common English words sound like dirty words when pronounced in the French fashion.

The wit combat of Beatrice and Benedick in *Much Ado About Nothing* is a merry war between two potential lovers, but it is also full of invective and slander. They go to great lengths to defend their unmarried state. The question that arises is whether the plotting to make them fall in love with each other and get married is really necessary. I think the play is set up in such a way that there is no possibility that the two will marry without some help from their friends.

The Roman style of *Julius Caesar* seems to be a deliberate attempt on Shakespeare's part to create a style suitable to his Roman subject matter. The play has one of the smallest vocabularies of any of his works, and it makes almost no use of figurative language. It has a great many monosyllabic (or near-monosyllabic) lines, and it also uses some old-fashioned rhetorical devices like apostrophe. Remember that the play is usually dated between *Henry V* and *Hamlet*.

Jaques in *As You Like It* functions as a satiric observer. Like Touchstone, the Clown, Jaques satirizes pastoral conventions and romantic assertions. He is definitely a malcontent, and proud of his melancholy humor, although it sometimes takes a sentimental turn. His seven ages of man speech is sour and cynical, but Duke Senior and his exiled court are entertained by Jaques's wit. The name, pronounced "Jakes," makes a continuing pun because it is also an Elizabethan word for a toilet.

Feste, the Clown, is Olivia's corrupter of words in *Twelfth Night*. His verbal dexterity is remarkable, ranging from puns and wordplay to double-talk and learned nonsense to outright parody. His histrionic skill in the role of Sir Topas, the Curate, who ministers to the "mad" Malvolio, is notable. He is full of mock quotations and satire on learning.

Hamlet as actor is only one of the ways of talking about his style. It is surprising how strong a connection there is between Hamlet and the contemporary theater. His advice to the players offers an intelligent commentary on Shakespeare's own theater. Hamlet seems self-conscious of his own ranting style, like a bad actor, and he can suddenly change to a more purposive discourse. After he has met with the ghost of his father, he is capable of putting on "an antic disposition" and playing mad as a form of self-protection.

There is a great deal of sex nausea in *Troilus and Cressida*. The Trojan War is represented as anti-heroic and anti-romantic. The play seems like a tragedy, but it has so much satirical invective in it that it is often called a comical satire. Pandarus, who is Cressida's uncle and go-between, speaks with sexual innuendo, and Cressida herself is a supremely ambivalent character. Ulysses calls her, unflatteringly, one of these "daughters of the game." The scurrilous Thersites does a good deal to promote a cynical view of both the war and the possibilities of love.

Like Falstaff in the *Henry IV* plays, Parolles, the man of words in *All's Well That Ends Well*, is a "miles gloriosus," a braggart but an errant coward. Everyone in the play recognizes him as a liar and a rogue, except for Bertram, who flees from his marriage to Helena. Parolles's language is extravagant (as is his dress too), and he misuses a number of italianate words that have nothing to do with the context. After his unmasking, he manages to survive by recognizing his own histrionic role and vowing that in the future he will be "Simply the thing I am."

Iago's "Ha! I like not that" (3.3.35) when he sees Cassio leaving Desdemona marks an important moment in the play. "Ha" in itself is a meaningless interjection, but the speaker can make it an emotionally loaded exclamation expressing surprise or wonder. Iago is an excellent actor, and he plays on Othello's credulousness, so that he soon picks up what is essentially Iago's word. Iago understands wonderfully well Othello's tragic vulnerability, and "Ha" marks his seduction by Iago.

Lucio functions as a calumniator in *Measure for Measure*, but he may also be an unpleasant truth-speaker. He is described in the cast of characters as a "fantastic," which means literally a creature of fantasy, but it also identifies him as extravagant, capricious, and bizarre. He slanders the absent Duke for no apparent reason, but he may also be providing us with special insights into the Duke's failings. He encourages Isabella to plead with Angelo to spare her brother, but he also refuses bail for Pompey when he is taken to prison.

Madness in *King Lear* is useful, stylistically, for broadening and deepening his role and providing him with a much wider range of emotions. The king comes to understand things that he took no notice of before, like the plight of "Poor naked wretches" (3.4.28). The Fool is Lear's closest companion in his madness, offering him a way to understand what has gone wrong with his previous perception of reality. At the very end of the play, Lear recovers from his madness, but he dies soon afterward. Interestingly, only act 4, scene 6 shows the king completely mad.

Insomnia troubles both Macbeth and Lady Macbeth. In their extreme guilt over the murder of King Duncan, they cannot sleep. More murders follow, but the Macbeths are never at peace with themselves. Lady Macbeth raises important questions about her husband's manliness, but the issue is never resolved in the play. At the end, Lady Macbeth goes mad and is troubled by images of blood, while her husband falls into a deep despair, regarding life as "a tale / Told by an idiot" (5.5.26–27).

In the symbolic contrast between the values of Egypt and Rome in *Antony and Cleopatra*, we need to remember that Antony is also a great Roman general as well as a lover. The Roman Antony is conceived in terms of Stoic values: strong self-control, a powerful sense of duty, and a seriousness of purpose. Antony is also manly. He struggles, unsuccessfully, against his dotage in Egypt, and he is well aware of his impending tragedy. His marriage to Octavia, Caesar's sister, is well-intentioned, but he is inexorably drawn to Cleopatra in Egypt.

*Timon of Athens* is perhaps not a fully finished play. It cultivates excess both in Timon's prosperity in the first part and his adversity in the second. This is a bitterly satirical play, full of invective about money and the exercise of political power. Many false suitors, like the Poet, the Painter, and the Jeweler, apply to Timon for money and gifts, and when he discovers an unlimited supply of gold in his exile, he is still extravagant in his bounty. Apemantus, the cynical truth-speaker, tries, unsuccessfully, to curb Timon's excesses.

Coriolanus is represented as a manly Roman warrior who despises the cowardly plebeians. When he returns from his bloody battle with the Volscians, he cannot compromise his own integrity to play a humble role so that he may be chosen consul. Volumnia, his dominating mother, pleads with him to be politic, but her son can only follow his own patrician values (that he has, of course, learned from his mother). There is a turn in the action when Coriolanus, at his mother's entreaty, agrees to spare Rome, but he knows it will be fatal to him.

Marina, Pericles's daughter in *Pericles*, is a super-romantic heroine, who, in her absolute innocence, plays a saintly role. In the overtly sexual brothel scenes in Mytilene, Marina not only preserves her virginity; she also converts all her clients, including Lysimachus, the Governor of Mytilene. At the end of the play, she manages, movingly, to revive her grieving father.

Imogen, the romance heroine of *Cymbeline*, resembles Marina in her innocence and purity. She maintains her love and devotion to her exiled husband, Posthumus Leonatus, in spite of a great many difficulties and improbabilities. She resists the powerful suit of the italianate villain, Iachimo. The labyrinthine plotting of the play, including a theophany of the God Jupiter and the ghosts of Leonatus's parents, is all resolved in the happy ending that fulfills the oracle.

In the chapter on *The Winter's Tale*, I consider the elaborate speech rhythms of the play that depart from the iambic pentameter pattern. The blank verse of this late play is very different from that of Shakespeare's earlier comedies. The dramatic speech rhythms override what we have come to expect from Shakespeare's blank verse. For example, there are many unexpected caesuras, or pauses, in the five-beat line, and there is liberal use of enjambment, or the continuation of the line beyond the five-beat ending. There is also abundant use of spondaic feet, with two accented syllables (rather than the iambic unaccented and accented foot) to imitate passionate speech.

Prospero's magical art in *The Tempest* is meant to be taken seriously as a way of understanding the play. Virtually everything happens by way of magic, including the shipwreck and the bringing together of Ferdinand and Miranda. Prospero does not use black magic, like Doctor Faustus in Marlowe's play. His knowledge comes from the intense study of books rather than from a compact with the devil. But any kind of magic is dangerous, and, at the end of the play, Prospero abandons his books and magical accoutrements in order to regain his essential humanity.

Cardinal Wolsey seems like a tragic character in Shakespeare's history play *Henry VIII*. He is a faithful servant of the king and does his bidding, including the divorce from his loving wife Katherine. Wolsey, the son of a butcher, is surrounded by his aristocratic enemies at court, whom he manages to outwit. Through a series of mistakes, however, Wolsey incurs the displeasure of the king and his fall is imminent. We sympathize with him in his adversity, as we also do with King Richard II.

The Jailer's Daughter in *The Two Noble Kinsmen* goes mad for her love of Palamon, and her mad style very much follows that of Ophelia in *Hamlet*. She is pretty and lyrical in her devotion to her lover, and she sings many songs. The Doctor, who comes to counsel her father, manages to cure her of her madness by the practical expedient of the nameless Wooer, who pretends to be Palamon, but has vigorous sexual intercourse with his paramour.

In the conclusion, I draw some general observations about Shakespeare's style. The main point is that Shakespeare is so varied in his plays that one cannot make easy generalizations. He doesn't repeat his successes; for example, he never writes another farce based on Plautus after the success of *The Comedy of Errors*, or another comedy strongly indebted to John Lyly after *Love's Labor's Lost*. Shakespeare draws on a wide variety of sources to construct his plays, especially Holinshed's *Chronicles* for the English history plays and Plutarch's *Lives* for the Roman plays, but one can pursue this matter further in the eight volumes of Geoffrey Bullough's *Narrative and Dramatic Sources of Shakespeare* (1957–1975). Shakespeare is especially skillful in creating convincing villains and satirical observers, a topic that I have developed in *Shakespeare's Villains* (2012). In his frequent soliloquies and asides, he explores the self-consciousness of his characters, a broad topic that is excellently discussed in A. C. Bradley's *Shakespearean Tragedy* (1904), which deals with the four major tragedies. A more modern discussion, strongly oriented to the theater, is in Harley Granville-Barker's various *Prefaces to Shakespeare* in six volumes (1927–1948).

Shakespeare's plays are often deliberately ambiguous in order to take advantage of unresolved dramatic conflict. For example, in *Julius Caesar*, Shakespeare's sympathies are divided between his compassion for the conspirators, especially Brutus, and his feeling that the party of Caesar must inevitably triumph. We have the impression in many plays that Shakespeare wants to have it both ways and avoid definitive judgments about his characters. In *Macbeth*, for example, the murderous protagonist begins the play with a moral sensitivity with which we cannot fail to be sympathetic. And what about Shylock in *The Merchant of Venice*? He is intent on a murderous revenge, but we also hear a lot about his cruel treatment by Antonio, the Christian, to whom Shylock is asked to lend money. As Shylock exclaims with so much ironic bitterness:

> "Fair sir, you spet on me on Wednesday last,
> You spurned me such a day, another time
> You called me dog; and for these courtesies
> I'll lend you thus much moneys?" (1.3.123–26)

In any close reading of Shakespeare's plays, we should be particularly attentive to the complexity of his writing. And we should not despair at not being able to "pin down" Shakespeare's style. For, like Cleopatra, its hallmark is "infinite variety" (2.2.238).

*Chapter One*

# Antipholus of Syracuse as Comic Hero in *The Comedy of Errors*

*The Comedy of Errors* is Shakespeare's only thorough imitation of Plautus, the prolific Roman comedy writer of the third and second centuries BCE. Shakespeare goes Plautus one better by doubling the twin masters and the twin servants, thus more than doubling the fun of mistaken identity. We must assume a kind of comic impenetrability in the play so that Antipholus of Syracuse and his servant, Dromio, can never ascertain, although there are clues in abundance, that they have found their lost brothers. I would like to speak about Antipholus of Syracuse as the ideal comic protagonist, because his great good fortune comes not from any intrinsic merit in himself but purely by chance and a willingness to accept, without too much questioning, all the good things that come his way. This lighthearted conception of your own identity is clearly comic, whereas in tragedies, such as Sophocles's *Oedipus*, identity is a serious and profound matter.

Antipholus of Syracuse, accompanied by his servant, Dromio, has been on a long search for his missing twin brother (and his mother too). In Ephesus in act I, scene 2, his quest seems hopeless:

I to the world am like a drop of water
That in the ocean seeks another drop,
Who, falling there to find his fellow forth,
Unseen, inquisitive, confounds himself.
So I, to find a mother and a brother,
In quest of them, unhappy [unlucky], lose myself. (1.2.35–40)

Antipholus seems melancholy and not very hopeful of succeeding in his search.

1

He meets the wrong Dromio (Dromio of Ephesus), who knows nothing of the money Antipholus has entrusted him with. He beats him, which is the usual way that difficult situations in farce are resolved. Antipholus fears that the town of Ephesus is a malign place and that he should leave as soon as possible:

> They say this town is full of cozenage:
> As nimble jugglers that deceive the eye,
> Dark-working sorcerers that change the mind,
> Soul-killing witches that deform the body,
> Disguisèd cheaters, prating mountebanks,
> And many suchlike liberties of sin.
> If it prove so, I will be gone the sooner. (1.2.97–103)

So the play does not begin comically. There are occurrences that Antipholus cannot explain and the town itself seems threatening.

But by act 2, scene 2, everything is about to change. However, Antipholus needs to beat the other Dromio, who knows nothing about what his master has said to Dromio of Ephesus. Antipholus assumes that his own servant is playing a practical joke on him. But the elaborate jesting on hair comes to a sudden end when Adriana, the wife of Antipholus of Ephesus, and her sister, Luciana, enter. Adriana has a long, humble speech declaring that her husband must be spending time with his girlfriend. Antipholus is genuinely puzzled by what is going on:

> Plead you to me, fair dame? I know you not.
> In Ephesus I am but two hours old,
> As strange unto your town as to your talk;
> Who, every word by all my wit being scanned,
> Wants wit in all one word to understand. (2.2.148–52)

So all the actors in the play are thoroughly bemused and think that everyone must be involved in a huge, practical joke. The questions everyone asks each other all have puzzling, mistaken answers.

Antipholus is sure that something strange is going on: "How can she thus then call us by our names, / Unless it be by inspiration?" (2.2.167–68), but he still attributes it to the witchcraft for which Ephesus is famous. Adriana is in no doubt that Antipholus is her husband, and her genuine affection gives him pause. He says aside:

> To me she speaks, she moves me for her theme;
> What, was I married to her in my dream?
> Or sleep I now, and think I hear all this?
> What error drives our eyes and ears amiss?
> Until I know this sure uncertainty,

I'll entertain the offered fallacy. (2.2.182–87)

This speech is at the heart of the comic assumptions of the play. Dreaming is added to witchcraft as an explanation of the mystery, and "error," in its Latin sense of a wandering of the mind, is now introduced as a way to solve the paradox, as expressed in the oxymoron "sure uncertainty."

Now the comedy takes an optimistic turn for Antipholus as he commits himself to accept the present reality, although he is sure that it is all a delusion ("the offered fallacy"). Antipholus makes what is essentially a comic choice: to play along with the delusion so long as it bestows rich benefits on him. A tragic protagonist would not let the question of his real identity slip by without making a heroic effort of finding out who he really is. His servant Dromio is not convinced:

> This is the fairyland. O spite of spites!
> We talk with goblins, owls, and sprites;
> If we obey them not, this will ensue:
> They'll suck our breath, or pinch us black and blue. (2.2.190–93)

Antipholus, however, cannot refuse Adriana's appealing invitation to have dinner (and probably sex) with her. In another aside, he declares his total commitment to the "offered fallacy":

> Am I in earth, in heaven, or in hell?
> Sleeping or waking, mad or well-advised?
> Known unto these, and to myself disguised?
> I'll say as they say, and persever so,
> And in this mist at all adventures go. (2.2.213–17)

There is no stopping Antipholus now, and he earnestly seeks to enjoy his new and inexplicable situation.

Antipholus's soliloquy at the beginning of act 4, scene 3 is entirely characteristic (but he, nevertheless, wants to escape from Ephesus as soon as possible before his good luck changes):

> There's not a man I meet but doth salute me
> As if I were their well-acquainted friend;
> And everyone doth call me by my name.
> Some tender money to me, some invite me;
> Some other give me thanks for kindnesses;
> Some offer me commodities to buy.
> Even now a tailor called me in his shop
> And showed me silks that he had bought for me,
> And therewithal took measure of my body.
> Sure, these are but imaginary wiles,
> And Lapland sorcerers inhabit here. (4.3.1–11)

Although Antipholus is convinced that these are tricks of his imagination ("imaginary wiles"), he still takes whatever is offered to him without any deeper questioning.

A Courtesan invites him to dinner, and it is evident that this is not the first dinner they have shared. Antipholus tries to exercise his righteous indignation: "Avoid, then, fiend! What tell'st thou me of supping? / Thou art, as you are all, a sorceress. / I conjure thee to leave me and be gone" (4.3.64–66). But the Courtesan is of a practical turn of mind and is not to be put off: "Give me the ring of mine you had at dinner, / Or, for my diamond, the chain you promised, / And I'll be gone, sir, and not trouble you" (4.3.70–72). Of course, these are all happenings that pertain to Antipholus of Ephesus when his wife barred him from entering his house for dinner.

All the misunderstandings of the play are cleared up in the dénouement in act 5, scene 1. Adriana says: "I see two husbands, or mine eyes deceive me" (5.1.332). We don't really know whether she means to express her good fortune or her bad, in the sense that two husband are double trouble. In addition to everything else, Egeon is no longer condemned to death, and he discovers that the Abbess is his long-lost wife, Emilia. Despite what we expect, neither Antipholus seems overjoyed to discover his long-lost brother, nor are the Dromio twins ecstatic either. Dromio of Ephesus says only: "Methinks you are my glass [mirror], and not my brother; / I see by you I am a sweet-faced youth" (5.1.418–19). At the end of the play, he graciously invites his brother to exit together with him: "We came into the world like brother and brother: / And now let's go hand in hand, not one before another" (5.1.426–27). We are waiting for the Antipholus twins to have some courteous concluding statement, but it doesn't occur.

*Chapter Two*

# The Satire on Learning in
# *Love's Labor's Lost*

Shakespeare seems to be enjoying himself in *Love's Labor's Lost* by making fun of rhetorical rules and principles. As Moth, Don Armado's page, says in an aside to the clown Costard: "They have been at a great feast of languages and stol'n the scraps" (5.1.37–38). This applies to Don Armado, described in the dramatis personae as a "fantastical Spaniard" and elsewhere as simply a braggart; Holofernes, the schoolmaster, also called the Pedant; and Nathaniel the Curate. These three characters generate a good deal of amusement in the play as they struggle with the intricacies of a rhetoric founded on Latin. Parson Evans in *The Merry Wives of Windsor* and the schoolmaster in *The Two Noble Kinsmen* both imitate Holofernes in their devotion to pedantry.

We see Holofernes and Nathaniel at their best in act 4, scene 2. They are at ease in their preoccupation with words, especially with words derived from Latin. They both speak with an emphasis on copiousness and amplification of discourse. For example, Holofernes speaks as if he were reading from a Latin dictionary. He cannot forgo any of the definitions. In his learned discourse on different types and ages of deer, Holofernes spares no detail: "The deer was, as you know, sanguis, in blood; ripe as the pomewater [a juicy apple], who now hangeth like a jewel in the ear of coelo, the sky, the welkin, the heaven; and anon falleth like a crab [crab apple] on the face of terra, the soil, the land, the earth" (4.2.3–7). Nathaniel, the curate, dutifully applauds his master's skill with synonyms: "Truly, Master Holofernes, the epithets are sweetly varied, like a scholar at the least" (4.2.8–9).

Holofernes waxes passionate in his objection to Constable Dull's contention that the animal was a pricket, or two-year-old red deer. He cannot contain his indignation at the ignorance of Dull, who is probably illiterate in any case:

Most barbarous intimation! Yet a kind of insinuation, as it were, in *via*, in way,
of explication; *facere* [to make], as it were, replication, or rather, *ostentare*, to
show, as it were, his inclination—after his undressed, unpolished, uneducated,
unpruned, untrained, or, rather, unlettered, or, ratherest, unconfirmed fashion—to insert again my *haud credo* for a deer. (4.2.13–20)

Dull, in his ignorance, takes the Latin "*haud credo*" to refer to an old grey
doe. Holofernes is hardly speaking English (or Latin either) but a mishmash
of the two with endless specifications.

He flourishes his superior learning over Dull, as the butt of these latinate,
insider jokes. Both Holofernes and Nathaniel lord it over the poor Dull, who
probably doesn't understand a word of what they are saying. Holofernes
exclaims scornfully: "Twice sod [soaked] simplicity, *bis coctus* [twice
cooked]! / O thou monster Ignorance, how deformed dost thou look!"
(4.2.23–24). Nathaniel goes into more detail, partly in hexameters, in his
disdain for Dull: "Sir, he hath never fed of the dainties that are bred in a
book. He hath not eat paper, as it were, he hath not drunk ink. His intellect is
not replenished. He is only an animal, only sensible in the duller parts"
(4.2.25–28). The two "book-men" (4.1.35)—Dull's word—are excessively
proud of themselves and thankful, "Which we of taste and feeling are, for
those parts that do fructify in us more than he" (4.1.29–30).

There is no room for modesty in these two pedants. As Don Armada calls
Holofernes, "Arts-man, preambulate [walk forth]. We will be singled from
the barbarous" (5.1.78–79). Holofernes speaks of his rhetorical endowments
with a singular innocence, as if he is just reporting the facts to the unlettered
world:

This is a gift that I have, simple, simple; a foolish extravagant spirit, full of
forms, figures, shapes, objects, ideas, apprehensions, motions, revolutions.
These are begot in the ventricle of memory, nourished in the womb of *pia
mater*, and delivered upon the mellowing of occasion. But the gift is good in
those in whom it is acute, and I am thankful for it. (4.2.66–73)

Holofernes is rather artless in his boasting. He is so immersed in the world of
latinate rhetoric that he has no self-consciousness at all about his relation to
the rest of the nonpedantic world.

Don Armada is not a pedant, but he nevertheless pairs well with Holofernes and Nathaniel in his ornate, euphuistic style (influenced by John
Lyly's *Euphues: The Anatomy of Wit*, 1579). He is not so specifically latinate
as the schoolmaster and the curate, but he follows the demands of rhetoric
with overbearing fullness. For example, in his letter to the king about Jaque-
netta and Costard, he answers his own questions, as orators were taught to do
in their orations:

The time When? About the sixth hour; when beasts most graze, birds best peck, and men sit down to that nourishment which is called supper. So much for the time When. Now for the ground Which? Which, I mean, I walked upon. It is ycleped [named] thy park. Then for the place Where? Where, I mean, I did encounter that obscene and most preposterous event, that draweth from my snow-white pen the ebon-colored ink, which here thou viewest, beholdest, surveyest, or see'st. But to the place Where? It standeth north-north-east and by east from the west corner of thy curious-knotted garden. (1.1.234–45)

There is an amusing copiousness and amplification in this letter. Don Armada doesn't hesitate to specify exactly (and more than exactly) what he wishes to say. Why do we need to know the precise place where he encounters the event he is writing about: "north-north-east and by east from the west corner of thy curious-knotted garden?" Don Armado is drunk with words, and he uses the same sort of synonymy as Holofernes does when he says "viewest, beholdest, surveyest, or see'st." Why not just "see'st?" He also refreshes the obsolete medieval word "ycleped" for "called." This is tedious but entertaining in its extravagance.

In the next scene (1.2), Don Armado meets his verbal match in his page, Moth. There is an elaborate play on words that has only an expressive meaning. Armado begins by asking his page:

*Armado.* How canst thou part sadness and melancholy, my tender juvenal?

*Moth.* By a familiar demonstration of the working, my tough signor.

*Armado.* Why tough signor? Why tough signor?

*Moth.* Why tender juvenal? Why tender juvenal?

*Armado.* I spoke it, tender juvenal, as a congruent epitheton appertaining to thy young days, which we may nominate tender.

*Moth.* And I, tough signor, as an appertinent title to your old time, which we may name tough. (1.2.7–17)

Moth suddenly blossoms as a skillful rhetorician, imitating—and parodying—his master. This passage bears no relation to the action of the play, but is there purely for our entertainment. This is what Don Armado calls later the "Sweet smoke of rhetoric" (3.1.63).

To return to act 1, scene 2, Don Armado's long soliloquy on love at the end of the scene obviously prepares us for what the king, Longaville, Dumaine, and especially Berowne will say later in the play (3.1 and, most elaborately, in 4.3). Don Armado seeks clarity of vision in his overspecifications about the workings of love:

> I do affect the very ground which is base, where her shoe (which is baser) guided by her foot (which is basest) doth tread. I shall be forsworn (which is a great argument of falsehood) if I love. And how can that be true love which is falsely attempted? Love is a familiar; Love is a devil. There is no evil angel but Love. Yet was Samson so tempted, and he had an excellent strength; yet was Solomon so seduced, and he had a very good wit. Cupid's butt-shaft is too hard for Hercules' club, and therefore too much odds for a Spaniard's rapier. (1.2.163–73)

We need to take seriously Don Armado's overly full speculations about the nature of love and his comparison of himself with famous lovers, since that is what *Love's Labor's Lost* is all about. He has an ardor that some of the more upper class lovers lack: "Adieu, valor; rust, rapier; be still, drum; for your manager is in love; yea, he loveth. Assist me some extemporal god of rhyme, for I am sure I shall turn sonnet. Devise, wit; write, pen; for I am for whole volumes in folio" (1.2.177–81).

Don Armado is more believable in his passion than Berowne and his fellow lords, whose love affair is put off for a year and day. The ladies are not convinced of their sincerity.

## Chapter Three

# Richard's Physical Deformities in
# *3 Henry VI* and *Richard III*

Richard of Gloucester's physical deformities are very much a part of his own thinking; he is acutely conscious of being foul and unappealing. If he is incapable of being a lover, he will make up for it by being powerful. There is a curious connection between his deformity and his unquenchable thirst for the crown, as if he were another Marlovian Tamburlaine. To be king by whatever means it takes is a superior goal to being merely sexually attractive.

Richard's long soliloquies in act 3, scene 2 and act 5, scene 6 of *3 Henry VI* are matched by his powerful opening soliloquy in *Richard III*. As one of Shakespeare's earliest villains (perhaps Aaron in *Titus Andronicus* is earlier), Richard is frankly aware of his own physical shortcomings. In describing himself, he even uses the word "chaos," the word for an amorphous, shapeless mass:

> Why, love forswore me in my mother's womb:
> And, for I should not deal in her soft laws,
> She did corrupt frail nature with some bribe,
> To shrink mine arm up like a withered shrub;
> To make an envious mountain on my back,
> Where sits deformity to mock my body;
> To shape my legs of an unequal size;
> To disproportion me in every part,
> Like to a chaos, or an unlicked bearwhelp
> That carries no impression like the dam. (3.2.153–62)

It is notable that Richard is so acutely aware of his own deformities, which he makes no effort to mitigate. These deformaties are mentioned by many other characters in this play and in *Richard III*.

9

Richard is emphatic in his certainty that love has "forsworn," or abandoned and renounced, him, already before he was born. Even if he cannot
attain the crown, he is sardonic about "What other pleasure can the world
afford" (3.2.147):

> I'll make my heaven in a lady's lap,
> And deck my body in gay ornaments
> And witch sweet ladies with my words and looks.
> O miserable thought! and more unlikely
> Than to accomplish twenty golden crowns! (3.2.148–52)

He repeats with no uncertain emphasis the impossibility of his being a lover:

> And am I then a man to be beloved?
> O monstrous fault, to harbor such a thought!
> Then, since this earth affords no joy to me,
> But to command, to check, to o'erbear such
> As are of better person than myself,
> I'll make my heaven to dream upon the crown,
> And, whiles I live, t' account this world but hell,
> Until my misshaped trunk that bears this head
> Be round impalèd with a glorious crown. (3.2.163–71)

He separates himself from the world that is of better appearance ("person")
than himself.

Richard uses his monstrous physical deformities to justify his duplicitous
villainy:

> Why, I can smile, and murder whiles I smile,
> And cry, "Content" to that which grieves my heart,
> And wet my cheeks with artificial tears,
> And frame my face to all occasions. (3.2.182–85)

Like most villains in Shakespeare, he is painfully truthful with himself, and
he lays out for us, with unabashed frankness, his course of conduct in both *3
Henry VI* and *Richard III*. He is proud of the fact that he "can add colors to
the chameleon, / Change shapes with Proteus for advantages, / And set the
murderous Machiavel to school" (3.2.191–93). In other words, he boasts that
he can out-machiavel the notorious Machiavelli, the source of evil in the
Renaissance. So now that we know Richard's motivation, we will not be
surprised or shocked by anything he does.

In another long soliloquy in act 5, scene 6, Richard reiterates his rejection
of love. He sees it clearly as a natural consequence of his physical deformity:

> Then, since the heavens have shaped my body so,

Let hell make crook'd my mind to answer it.
I have no brother, I am like no brother;
And this word "love," which graybeards call divine,
Be resident in men like one another
And not in me: I am myself alone. (5.6.78–83)

He speaks like Iago in *Othello*. He is an atheist, freed from the prohibitions that restrict other men. His brother Clarence is doomed, but so are all the others who stand between him and the crown: "Clarence, thy turn is next, and then the rest, / Counting myself but bad till I be best" (5.6.90–91). Richard seems certain of obtaining the crown by killing all that stands in his way. As he says in an aside after kissing his brother King Edward: "To say the truth, so Judas kissed his master, / And cried 'All hail!' whenas he meant all harm" (5.7.33–34). Richard, the atheist, gleefully adopts the role of Judas, whom he sees as a diabolical prototype.

Richard's soliloquies and asides in *3 Henry VI* lead directly into his soliloquy at the beginning of *Richard III*, which continues the earlier play as if the two plays were designed to follow each other. "Grim-visaged war" might caper "nimbly in a lady's chamber / To the lascivious pleasing of a lute" (1.1.9, 12–13), but not Richard, who was meant for other actions:

But I, that am not shaped for sportive tricks
Nor made to court an amorous looking glass;
I, that am rudely stamped, and want love's majesty
To strut before a wanton ambling nymph;
I, that am curtailed of this fair proportion,
Cheated of feature by dissembling Nature,
Deformed, unfinished, sent before my time
Into this breathing world scarce half made up,
And that so lamely and unfashionable
That dogs bark at me as I halt by them;
Why, I, in this weak piping time of peace,
Have no delight to pass away the time,
Unless to spy my shadow in the sun
And descant on my own deformity. (1.1.14–27)

Richard seems to delight in his own deformity, something that sets him apart—and renders him superior—to other men. By his frankness, Richard endears himself to the audience. There is not the slightest attempt at conceal-ment. The conclusion is obvious:

And therefore, since I cannot prove a lover
To entertain these fair well-spoken days,
I am determinèd to prove a villain
And hate the idle pleasures of these days. (1.1.28–31)

Richard is resolved to make a firm dichotomy between being a lover and being a villain.

His successful wooing of Lady Anne in the next scene does not at all contradict this assumption, but it only proves how powerful and calculating a villain Richard is. He is impervious to Anne's insults—"thou lump of foul deformity" (1.2.57), "diffused [shapeless] infection of a man" (1.2.78), "hedgehog" (1.2.102), and "toad" (1.2.147)—and relentlessly pursues his wooing. When Anne exits, Richard is contemptuous at her being won so easily: "Was ever woman in this humor wooed? / Was ever woman in this humor won? / I'll have her, but I will not keep her long" (1.2.227–29). The last sentence means that he plans to have her murdered when she no longer serves his turn. Richard's "Ha!" (1.2.238), like Iago's "Ha" in *Othello* (3.3.35), is an expression of astonishment, and also a word vindicating his triumphant role-playing. He congratulates himself that he has maneuvered Anne into loving him, "whose all not equals Edward's moi'ty? / On me, that halts and am misshapen thus?" (1.2.249–50).

The absurdity of the present situation launches Richard into his best sardonic style:

> My dukedom to a beggarly denier,
> I do mistake my person all this while.
> Upon my life, she finds, although I cannot,
> Myself to be a marv'lous proper man.
> I'll be at charges for a looking glass
> And entertain a score or two of tailors
> To study fashions to adorn my body.
> Since I am crept in favor with myself,
> I will maintain it with some little cost. (1.2.251–59)

Richard is thoroughly enjoying his triumph over Anne. He does not for a moment believe that he has suddenly become "a marv'lous proper man" or wondrously handsome, or that he has mistaken his "person," or appearance. His glee is based on the credulousness and blindness of Anne. He feels fully justified in gloating over his conquest.

In addition to his own keen dwelling on his deformity, Richard is seen by others throughout these two plays as spectacularly ugly, misshapen, and monstrous. This repeated imagery should certainly figure into the way Richard is represented on stage. He is most frequently referred to in animal images: of the boar, which is his heraldic crest, and of the hedgehog, toad, and spider.

Already at the end of *2 Henry VI*, Young Clifford calls him "Foul stigmatic" (5.1.215). This is an unusual word in Shakespeare, used only in this play and in *3 Henry VI*, when Queen Margaret curses Richard and calls him "a foul misshapen stigmatic, / Marked by the Destinies to be avoided, / As venom toads, or lizards' dreadful stings" (2.2.136–38). "Stigmatic" refers to a criminal "stigmatized" or branded with a hot iron, as Richard is branded or stamped with various deformities, including a hunchback. In many places he is called "crookback." There are various references in these plays to Richard's having been born with teeth. As King Henry says in *3 Henry VI* before Richard stabs him: "Teeth hadst thou in thy head when thou wast born, / To signify thou cam'st to bite the world" (5.6.53–54). And in *Richard III*, the young Duke of York, King Edward's son—soon to be murdered in the Tower—says of Richard: "Marry, they say my uncle grew so fast / That he could gnaw a crust at two hours old" (2.4.27–28).

For a more continuous representation of Richard as a monster or prodigy, we should look at the scene in *Richard III* in which he is cursed by Queen Margaret. Speaking aside at the back of the stage, she calls him a "cacodemon" (1.3.143), or evil spirit, a word used only this once in Shakespeare. When she speaks with Richard, she addresses him as "dog" (1.3.215) and lashes out against him: "Thou elvish-marked, abortive, rooting hog! / Thou that wast sealed in thy nativity / The slave of nature and the son of hell!" (1.3.227–29). She warns Queen Elizabeth:

> Why strew'st thou sugar on that bottled [swollen] spider
> Whose deadly web ensnareth thee about?
> Fool, fool, thou whet'st a knife to kill thyself.
> The day will come that thou shalt wish for me
> To help thee curse this poisonous bunch-backed toad. (1.3.241–45)

Admittedly, Margaret is bitter against everyone, but she can only conceive of Richard, who slew her husband, as a diabolical force.

*Chapter Four*

# The Sardonic Aaron in
# *Titus Andronicus*

*Titus Andronicus* may be Shakespeare's earliest tragedy, which makes the figure of Aaron the Moor especially important. He provides a model for Shakespeare's later villains, especially for such figures as Richard III and Iago. I am thinking particularly of how these villains resemble the Vice in medieval morality plays. Aaron is sportive, merry, and ingenious in his evil-doing. He takes pride in the cleverness of his plotting, as if he were an artist of malevolence. "Sardonic" is a good word for Aaron and for other villains because it implies that they are not satanic or devilish in their ill deeds but mocking and cynical. For the most part, they seem deprived of a con-science—although Aaron genuinely loves his black baby. It is hard to explain how much satisfaction they take from being laughing villains.

We begin act 2 with Aaron's long, vaunting, Marlovian soliloquy, in which he lays claim to being a heroic figure:

> Then, Aaron, arm thy heart, and fit thy thoughts
> To mount aloft with thy imperial mistress,
> And mount her pitch, whom thou in triumph long
> Hast prisoner held, fettered in amorous chains. (2.1.12–15)

Like Marlowe's Tamburlaine, Aaron is prepared for great exploits.

His first action is to manipulate Demetrius and Chiron, Tamora's sons, into killing Bassianus and raping and disfiguring Lavinia, his wife and Tit-us's daughter. Aaron goes about his work with grossly sexual puns, remind-ing us of Shakespeare's earliest comedies:

> *Aaron.* Why, then, it seems, some certain snatch or so

Would serve your turns.

*Chiron.* Ay, so the turn were served.

*Demetrius.* Aaron, thou hast hit it.

*Aaron.* Would you had hit it too,

Then should not we be tired with this ado. (2.1.95–98)

"Snatch" probably has its modern slang meaning, "turn" refers to the turn in bed, and "hit it" is a jesting term from archery. Aaron's intervention in Demetrius and Chiron's quarrel is an act of "policy and stratagem" (2.1.104). His digging a hole for the murdered body of Bassianus; his trapping Titus's sons, Quintus and Martius, in that hole; and his burying a bag of gold nearby to implicate them in that murder is all a successful and cunning plot, and, in Aaron's words, "A very excellent piece of villainy" (2.3.7).

Aaron's most ingenious piece of villainy is to persuade Titus to chop off his hand and to send it to the king to save his two sons from execution. Titus is even grateful to Aaron for his intervention: "With all my heart, I'll send the Emperor my hand. / Good Aaron, wilt thou help to chop it off?" (3.1.160–61). We see Aaron cutting off Titus's hand right on stage, and he has an informative aside:

> If that be called deceit, I will be honest,
> And never whilst I live deceive men so:
> But I'll deceive you in another sort,
> And that you'll say, ere half an hour pass. (3.1.188–91)

Titus never sees his sons alive again, and he receives only their severed heads and his own hand back. Aaron is delighted in the extreme with his clever plot:

> O, how this villainy
> Doth fat me with the very thoughts of it!
> Let fools do good, and fair men call for grace,
> Aaron will have his soul black like his face. (3.1.202–5)

"Fat," meaning to nourish, is unusual as a verb in Shakespeare. Aaron feeds on his own malice.

Aaron's black baby provides a redeeming feature for him, and he defends it with great vigor. The Nurse presents the child as "A joyless, dismal, black, and sorrowful issue! / Here is the babe, as loathsome as a toad / Amongst the fair-faced breeders of our clime" (4.2.66–68). Aaron is resounding in his rejection of the Nurse's argument: "Zounds, ye whore! Is black so base a hue? / Sweet blowse [ruddy, fat-faced wench], you are a beauteous blossom, sure" (4.2.71–72). Aaron's ironic alliteration does not bode well for the Nurse—and this is surely an early expression of the black-is-beautiful theme. With Tamora's sons, Aaron is brutally slangy:

*Demetrius.* Villain, what hast thou done?

*Aaron.* That which thou canst not undo.

*Chiron.* Thou hast undone our mother.

*Aaron.* Villain, I have done thy mother. (4.2.73–76)

This is the only use in Shakespeare of "done" as a sexual term. Aaron waxes eloquent with references to Enceladus (a Titan), to Alcides (Hercules), and to Mars, the god of war, to put down Tamora's sons and to cow them into submission:

> What, what, ye sanguine, shallow-hearted boys!
> Ye white-limed walls! Ye alehouse painted signs!
> Coal black is better than another hue,
> In that it scorns to bear another hue,
> For all the water in the ocean
> Can never turn the swan's black legs to white,
> Although she lave them hourly in the flood. (4.2.97–103)

Aaron continues to expatiate on the black-is-beautiful theme, and his vigor of speech is notable in this early tragedy. It looks forward to Richard, Duke of Gloucester.

Aaron's plotting at this point silences Demetrius and Chiron. He suddenly kills the Nurse, with colloquial and jokey exclamations: "Wheak, wheak! / So cries a pig preparèd to the spit" (4.2.146–47). Is that the sound a pig makes when it is slaughtered? It hardly matters, since Aaron is now riding high on an energetic climax. His explanations to Tamora's sons seem hardly necessary: "O, lord, sir, 'tis a deed of policy! / Shall she live to betray this guilt of ours? / A long-tongued babbling gossip? No, lords, no" (4.2.149–51). "Policy" is the villain's word par excellence in Shakespeare. It is interesting how vividly Aaron's words define the Nurse's brief role in the play.

When Aaron is captured by Lucius and the army of the Goths, his final confessions are full of a bizarre glee at his extraordinary success as a villain. Although he is a confirmed atheist, Aaron insists on Lucius's oath that he will promise to bring up his black baby before he will say anything about his exploits. Again, Aaron's speech is vigorously colloquial and slangy to express his enjoyment at all the mischief he has done. He reports what actually happened with Lavinia. Demetrius and Chiron "cut thy sister's tongue and ravished her, / And cut her hands, and trimmed her as thou sawest" (5.1.92–93). "Trimmed" is an unusual word, a grossly comic word, and Lucius is shocked: "O detestable villain! Call'st thou that trimming?" (5.1.94). Aaron is obviously enjoying his confession, especially the sense of horror it provokes in Lucius: "Why, she was washed, and cut, and trimmed, and 'twas / Trim sport for them which had the doing of it" (5.1.95–96). Aaron is punning on the word "trim," which usually means nice or pretty. He is reveling in his heavy irony.

Aaron's final triumph is in his report of how Titus Andronicus asked him to cut off his hand in order to free his two sons from execution. It was all so supremely pointless that Aaron cannot control his mirth: "I played the cheater [escheator] for thy father's hand, / And when I had it drew myself apart, / And almost broke my heart with extreme laughter" (5.1.111–13). And, again, when Titus got his hand back with the heads of his two sons, Aaron could hardly restrain himself:

> I pried me through the crevice of a wall,
> When for his hand he had his two sons' heads;
> Beheld his tears and laughed so heartily
> That both mine eyes were rainy like to his. (5.1.114–17)

This is Aaron's "sport" (5.1.118), a word much used by Iago.

Aaron is unrepentant. His recital of his deeds is a bravura piece for him, and these are certainly his most important speeches in the play. His gleeful villainy is boundless and unquenchable:

> But, I have done a thousand dreadful things
> As willingly as one would kill a fly,
> And nothing grieves me heartily indeed,
> But that I cannot do ten thousand more. (5.1.141–44)

The mention of killing a fly recalls the strange mad scene of act 3, scene 2. Aside from his devotion to his black baby, Aaron is thoroughly diabolical, in a way that is different from Shakespeare's subsequent villains. He delights in tormenting Lucius:

> If there be devils, would I were a devil,
> To live and burn in everlasting fire,
> So I might have your company in hell,
> But to torment you with my bitter tongue! (5.1.147–50)

But remember that Aaron is an atheist who doesn't believe in hell or devils. This is, therefore, a purely speculative projection of Aaron's diabolical nature.

## Chapter Five

# Who Tames Whom in
# *The Taming of the Shrew*?

Shakespeare's *The Taming of the Shrew* is an early comedy that raises paradoxical questions. It is ostensibly a "shrew" play following in the tradition of other "shrew" plays with heroines that are "froward," "curst," and "shrewish," favorite words for Kate in Shakespeare's play. But we must also think of this play in its context, written around the time of *The Comedy of Errors*, *Love's Labor's Lost*, *The Two Gentlemen of Verona*, and *Romeo and Juliet*. It is wrong, I think, to believe that Shakespeare is suddenly a confirmed misogynist in *The Taming of the Shrew*, whereas in other plays of this period his women are intelligent, sprightly, witty, as well as forceful and independent. It's a real question, I believe, to ask who tames whom in this play or what taming is all about. Already in act 3, scene 2, Gremio is claiming that "Petruchio is Kated" (3.2.244), meaning he has met his match.

Petruchio is identified as a fortune-hunter from the beginning of the play. He tells his friend Hortensio that "wealth is burthen of my wooing dance" (1.2.67). He means to "wive it wealthily in Padua; / If wealthily, then happily in Padua" (1.2.74–75). It doesn't matter if his bride is "foul" (ugly), "old," "curst and shrewd," and "rough," so long as she has an attractive dowry. He has a specific plan to win Kate by contradicting everything she says and insisting on her sweetness and obedience—in other words, he plans to tame her. The word is used to refer to Petruchio's intention to reeducate Kate, to reform her to the conventional expectations of a good wife.

As he tells us in a soliloquy in act 4, scene 1, the taming process is based on falconry, the way a wild hawk, or "haggard," is meticulously trained to hunt game. Petruchio is confident of his ability to transform Kate into an obedient wife. He is "politic," a word closely associated with politicians like Polonius in *Hamlet*, and he thinks of himself as a kind of king when he says:

21

"Thus have I politicly begun my reign, / And 'tis my hope to end successfully" (4.1.177–78). He refers to Kate as his "falcon" (4.1.179), who is now
hungry ("sharp and passing empty"), but she will not be fed until she "stoop"
(4.1.180), or swoop down onto the lure.

That is not all that Petruchio intends to do; he will also prevent Kate from
sleeping until she is properly trained:

> Another way I have to man my haggard,
> To make her come and know her keeper's call,
> That is, to watch her [keep her awake] as we watch these kites
> That bate and beat and will not be obedient.
> She eat no meat today, nor none shall eat.
> Last night she slept not, nor tonight she shall not. (4.1.182–87)

This animal taming seems cruel, but we know that Petruchio is engaging in
macho, boasting about his skill: "This is a way to kill a wife with kindness"
(4.1.197). We need to remember that he suffers all of the privations of Kate.
He is as deeply embedded in the taming process as Kate is.

To return to Petruchio and Kate's initial encounter in act 2, scene 1: Kate
shows herself to be witty and boldly sexual in her dialogue with Petruchio.
She is no pushover as Petruchio imagined. Their give-and-take is laced with
overt sexual references:

*Kate.* What is your crest? A coxcomb [a fool's cap]?

*Petruchio.* A combless cock, so Kate will be my hen.

*Kate.* No cock of mine; you crow too like a craven [coward].

*Petruchio.* Nay, come, Kate, come, you must not look so sour.

*Kate.* It is my fashion when I see a crab [crab apple]. (2.1.223–27)

Kate is not to be put down, despite Petruchio's bravado and his clearly stated
intent: "For I am born to tame you, Kate, / And bring you from a wild Kate to
a Kate / Conformable as other household Kates" (2.1.269–71). Kate's interest is engaged in this wooing scene. Although she may be offended by
Petruchio's male posturing, she is attracted by no one else in the play.

After her marriage, Kate suffers grievously in Petruchio's country house,
in what should be her honeymoon, but Petruchio suffers with her, going
without food and sleep. The marriage is not yet consummated. We sense that
Kate is becoming more polite and kind in act 4, scene 1. When Petruchio
strikes a servant without much cause, Kate apologizes for him: "Patience, I
pray you. 'Twas a fault unwilling" (4.1.145). Her choleric testiness is being

reduced, and, in this respect, Petruchio's taming has an educational function. By act 4, scene 3, Kate is becoming humble:

> What, did he marry me to famish me?
> Beggars that come unto my father's door,
> Upon entreaty have a present alms;
> If not, elsewhere they meet with charity.
> But I, who never knew how to entreat
> Nor never needed that I should entreat,
> Am starved for meat, giddy for lack of sleep,
> With oaths kept waking and with brawling fed.
> And that which spites me more than all these wants,
> He does it under name of perfect love. (4.3.3–12)

One would say that Kate is growing up and beginning to experience the world for what it is. She never aroused the audience's emotional reactions before, and we are beginning to feel sorry for her.

The peripeteia, or turn in the action, begins at the end of this scene. Petruchio seems to be carried away in his testing (or taming) of Kate to such an extent that he wants to control reality. He seems to contradict his wife, merely for sport, about what time it is:

> It shall be seven ere I go to horse.
> Look what I speak or do or think to do,
> You are still crossing it. Sirs, let't alone:
> I will not go today, and ere I do,
> It shall be what o'clock I say it is. (4.3.189–93)

All Kate said was "'tis almost two" (4.3.187).

This game of contradictions reaches its climax in act 4, scene 5. They are on the road to Padua to Kate's father's house, but Petruchio wants to triumph over Kate in every minute aspect of their relation and show her who is boss. Their dialogue is a delightful panoply of perverse suppositions:

*Petruchio.* Come on, a God's name, once more toward our father's.

Good Lord, how bright and goodly shines the moon.

*Kate.* The moon? The sun. It is not moonlight now.

*Petruchio.* I say it is the moon that shines so bright.

*Kate.* I know it is the sun that shines so bright.

*Petruchio.* Now, by my mother's son, and that's myself,

It shall be moon or star or what I list,

Or ere I journey to your father's house. (4.5.1–8)

Petruchio seems here to have overplayed his role as master, and Hortensio gives Kate just the clue she needs to challenge him: "Say as he says or we shall never go" (4.5.11).

From here to the end of the play, Kate understands that being a wife is a social role that she must play according to conventional expectations. She now agrees with her husband: "Forward, I pray, since we have come so far, / And be it moon or sun or what you please" (4.5.12–13). Petruchio still wants to show his mastery—"I say it is the moon"—but Kate undercuts him by playing the marriage game of the obedient wife: "I know it is the moon" (4.5.16). Petruchio can no longer dictate the nature of reality to his cunning wife. It is no use for him to insist that "it is the blessèd sun" because Kate is ready to answer him in all of his mind games:

> Then God be blessed, it is the blessèd sun.
> But sun it is not when you say it is not,
> And the moon changes even as your mind.
> What you will have it named, even that it is,
> And so it shall be so for Katherine. (4.5.18–22)

Hortensio's aside at this point is ambiguous: "Petruchio, go thy ways. The field is won" (4.5.23). Does this mean that Petruchio's taming is now a complete success, or does it also mean that Kate has finally understood what is involved in playing the role of obedient wife? It looks as if, as Gremio observed earlier, "Petruchio is Kated" (3.2.245).

From here to the end of the play, Petruchio and Kate appear as a loving married couple, kissing and in good humor. In act 5, scene 2, they win an enormous wager based on whose wife will come promptly at her husband's call. Surprisingly, Bianca and Lucentio and Hortensio and his widow lose this bet, although we certainly could not have predicted this at the beginning of the play. Kate's long and submissive speech at the end of this scene is definitely not ironic. She means literally everything she says about the expected duties of an obedient, early English wife; in fact, she repeats conventional clichés from the marriage manuals:

> Thy husband is thy lord, thy life, thy keeper,
> Thy head, thy sovereign—one that cares for thee,
> And for thy maintenance commits his body
> To painful labor both by sea and land,
> To watch the night in storms, the day in cold,
> Whilst thou li'st warm at home, secure and safe;
> And craves no other tribute at thy hands

But love, fair looks, and true obedience:
Too little payment for so great a debt. (5.2.146–54)

We don't hear anything we don't already know, but Kate takes the argument to its ultimate, physiological basis when she says:

Why are our bodies soft and weak and smooth,
Unapt to toil and trouble in the world,
But that our soft conditions [qualities] and our hearts
Should well agree with our external parts? (5.2.165–68)

At the very end, her advice to Bianca and Hortensio's widow is extraordinarily submissive:

Then vail your stomachs [pride], for it is no boot,
And place your hands below your husband's foot,
In token of which duty, if he please,
My hand is ready, may it do him ease. (5.2.176–79)

Kate makes sure not to leave anything out in her declaration of wifely obedience. She knows exactly what to say and how to play her part. Petruchio's last speech begins: "Come, Kate, we'll to bed" (5.2.184). Is their marriage finally consummated at this point? We don't really know, but it is clear that Petruchio and his loving wife fare better than Sly and his supposed wife in the Induction.

*Chapter Six*

# The Conventions of Romantic Love in
# *The Two Gentlemen of Verona*

*The Two Gentlemen of Verona* is an early comedy, written shortly after *The Comedy of Errors* and *Love's Labor's Lost* and, perhaps, after *The Taming of the Shrew*. It develops themes and aspects of romantic love that will be more fully and more successfully fulfilled in the comedies that follow, like *A Midsummer Night's Dream* and *Much Ado About Nothing*. But Valentine and Proteus, the two gentlemen lovers of Verona, also strongly resemblance the disconsolate Romeo of the early part of *Romeo and Juliet*, a play that was written around the same time as *The Two Gentlemen of Verona*. Critics have objected to the artifice of the love action, particularly at the end of the play, when Proteus is so quickly forgiven for his perfidy and his friend, Valentine, is so carried away by the ideals of friendship: "All that was mine in Silvia I give thee" (5.4.83). It is difficult to accept the fact that the play takes the conventions of romantic love so literally and so unnaturalistically. But Shakespeare is only following the lead of the innumerable italianate stories he had read, especially the Portuguese Jorge de Montemayor's *Diana Enamorada* (1542).

The devotion of Proteus to Julia is established in the first scene of the play, but his departing friend, Valentine, is contemptuous of romantic love: he calls it "fond [or foolish] desire" (1.1.52). After Valentine leaves the stage to depart for Milan, Proteus has a soliloquy that both celebrates being in love and expresses his awareness of its pains:

> He after honor hunts, I after love.
> He leaves his friends to dignify them more,
> I leave myself, my friends, and all, for love.
> Thou, Julia, thou hast metamorphized me,

> Made me neglect my studies, lose my time,
> War with good counsel, set the world at nought,
> Made wit with musing weak, heart sick with thought. (1.1.63–69)

It is almost as if Proteus agrees with his scornful friend about the dangers of love. This scene suggests that the play will take up the love versus friendship theme, but this topic is not fully developed in the course of the play.

In the next scene, Julia seems more fervently in love than Proteus. Even though she tears up his letter, she passionately seeks to recover the pieces. She comments petulantly: "Fie, fie, how wayward is this foolish love, / That, like a testy babe, will scratch the nurse, / And presently, all humbled, kiss the rod!" (1.2.57–59). There seems to be a persistent separation between the male and female lovers in Shakespeare's comedies: the women are consistently more personal and more passionate.

Falling in love proceeds swiftly in this play. By the next scene, Valentine is suddenly in love with Silvia, the daughter of the Duke of Milan. His clown/servant, Speed, offers a description of his love melancholy that looks forward to Romeo's being smitten by Rosaline in *Romeo and Juliet*. Valentine, like his friend, Proteus, is now "metamorphized with a mistress" (2.1.31–32). Proteus's word "metamorphized" is repeated from 1.1.66 so that the two lovers are represented symmetrically. Valentine has

> learned, like Sir Proteus, to wreathe your arms, like a malcontent; to relish a love song, like a robin redbreast; to walk alone, like one that had the pestilence; to sigh, like a schoolboy that had lost his A B C; to weep, like a young wench that had buried her grandam; to fast, like one that takes diet; to watch [stay awake], like one that fears robbing; to speak puling [complainingly], like a beggar at Hallowmas. (2.1.20–27)

This catalogue of the authentic signs of love melancholy will serve as a template for all Shakespeare's comedies.

In his ardor for Silvia, Valentine as lover exceeds Proteus as lover of Julia, and it is interesting how the two gentlemen of Verona are developed as a matching pair. Valentine, the scoffer of love, is now doing

> penance for contemning Love,
> Whose high imperious thoughts have punished me
> With bitter fasts, with penitential groans,
> With nightly tears, and daily heartsore sighs;
> For, in revenge of my contempt of Love,
> Love hath chased sleep from my enthrallèd eyes,
> And made them watchers of mine own heart's sorrow. (2.4.129–35)

Love is personified—the god Cupid—as a "mighty lord" (2.4.136) who plays an active role in human affairs. In this early comedy, Shakespeare closely follows the conventions of romantic love. But even Proteus is astounded by the "braggardism" (2.4.164) of Valentine's speech.

In this same scene, however, Proteus is suddenly madly in love with Valentine's Silvia, which just goes to show how capricious and arbitrary love is. Act 2, scene 6 is devoted to Proteus's long love soliloquy, which now outdoes Valentine's declarations. Proteus is amply aware of his "threefold perjury" (2.6.5) to Julia and to Valentine, but an irresistible force drives him on:

> Julia I lose, and Valentine I lose.
> If I keep them, I needs must lose myself;
> If I lose them, thus find I by their loss
> For Valentine, myself, for Julia, Silvia.
> I to myself am dearer than a friend,
> For love is still most precious in itself. (2.6.19–24)

Love shows his tyranny here because it leads to slandering Valentine and declaring that both Valentine and Julia are dead. Of course, Proteus's vigorous protestations have no effect on the deep-sworn love of Silvia for Valentine.

In the final scene, Proteus goes beyond the conventions of romantic love in threatening to rape Silvia:

> Nay, if the gentle spirit of moving words
> Can no way change you to a milder form,
> I'll woo you like a soldier, at arms' end,
> And love you 'gainst the nature of love—force ye. (5.4.55–58)

Proteus sounds like the military Tarquin in *The Rape of Lucrece*, but we are sure that rape can never be a part of a romantic love comedy. Valentine, now an exiled outlaw, is there to intervene. We are astonished at how quickly the apologetic Proteus is forgiven—and even more astonished at Valentine's generosity: "All that was mine in Silvia I give thee" (5.4.83). But, as in *A Midsummer Night's Dream*, all is beneficially sorted out, and the play ends happily. As Valentine declares in his final lines:

> Come, Proteus; 'tis your penance but to hear
> The story of your loves discoverèd.
> That done, our day of marriage shall be yours;
> One feast, one house, one mutual happiness. (5.4.171–74)

We are not meant to take seriously the many perturbations and betrayals that are entwined in the love action.

## Chapter Seven

# The Portentous Tragedy of
# *Romeo and Juliet*

*Romeo and Juliet* is a tragedy from Shakespeare's mid-career. It is usually dated 1599, shortly before *Hamlet*. One of the first things we notice about the play is the abundance of rhyme, in couplets, quatrains (rhyming abab), and in a few fourteen-line sonnets. The frequent use of rhyme is associated with Shakespeare's early comedies, such as *A Midsummer Night's Dream*. The quantity of rhyming in *Romeo and Juliet* may be appropriate for its lyric presentation of love, but it still seems old-fashioned in relation to Shakespeare's development as a dramatist.

The play also seems unusual in its opening Prologue, which carefully lays out the way the action will unfold. There is a strong emphasis on fate: "From forth the fatal loins of these two foes / A pair of star-crossed lovers take their life" (0.5–6). Everything seems to depend on the longstanding feud between the Capulets and the Montagues rather than on the chosen destinies of the protagonists. Their love is "death-marked" (0.9) even before the play begins. There is a problem here for our understanding of Shakespearean tragedy, which must depend on free will and capacity for choice in individuals. We bridle at the idea that their fates are sealed and that they are doomed before the play even starts. That doesn't seem very tragic. We could well ask if we need this Prologue (there is another Prologue before act 2). What function does it serve in the tragedy? At the end of the play, there is a kind of conclusion to the opening Prologue in what the Prince, old Capulet, and old Montague say (5.3.287f).

*Romeo and Juliet* opens like one of Shakespeare's early comedies—*The Comedy of Errors*, for example—with elaborate and extended punning dialogue between Sampson and Gregory, servants of the house of Capulet. They are joined a bit further on by Abram and Balthasar, servants of the house of Montague. I quote the opening lines as a sample of the way the play begins:

*Sampson.* Gregory, on my word, we'll not carry coals [submit to insults].

*Gregory.* No, for then we should be colliers.

*Sampson.* I mean, and [if] we be in choler, we'll draw.

*Gregory.* Ay, while you live, draw your neck out of collar [hangman's noose]. (1.1.1–5)

The style is unlike the kinds of plays Shakespeare was writing around this time.

At the entrance of Tybalt, of the house of Capulet, the quarrel suddenly turns threatening: "What, art thou drawn among these heartless hinds? / Turn thee, Benvolio; look upon thy death" (1.168–69). Benvolio, a Montague, has been trying to prevent the servants from fighting. Notice how Tybalt, the swordsman, always speaks in a slightly ridiculous heroic style. "Heartless hinds" ("cowardly menials") is an elevated phrase, hardly consonant with ordinary speech. As the play progresses, Tybalt seems to be the only one who takes the feud seriously and literally. When Romeo is at the Capulet ball, where he falls in love with Juliet, old Capulet doesn't seem to mind his presence, but the fiery Tybalt is enflamed beyond measure:

What! Dares the slave
Come hither, covered with an antic face [Romeo's mask],
To fleer and scorn at our solemnity?
Now, by the stock and honor of my kin,
To strike him dead I hold it not a sin. (1.5.57–61)

Tybalt, with his overwrought style, seems out of place in this enjoyable scene. Old Capulet is more than perturbed by his nephew's aggressive behavior. He calls him "a saucy boy" (1.5.85) and a "princox" (1.5.88)—a strong word for a rude and impertinent adolescent (and used only this once in Shakespeare). Tybalt withdraws, but he predicts tragic consequences: "this intrusion shall, / Now seeming sweet, convert to bitt'rest gall" (1.5.93–94).

From everything we can understand about the play, Tybalt seems to be at the heart of the tragedy in *Romeo and Juliet*. In the first scene, he answers the peaceable Benvolio with swordsman's rhetoric: "What, drawn, and talk of peace? I hate the word / As I hate hell, all Montagues, and thee. / Have at thee, coward!" (1.1.72–74). For a character who is so important in the development of the tragedy, Tybalt is represented as a ridiculous figure, which makes for an incongruity between cause and effect. In the crucial act 3, scene

1, where Mercutio is killed by Tybalt and the tragedy begins in earnest, Tybalt in Mercutio's eyes is a blustering, pretentious over-actor. He answers Tybalt's question, "What wouldst thou have with me?" (3.1.77), with comic disdain: "Good King of Cats, nothing but one of your nine lives" (3.1.78–79). He doesn't see Tybalt as a serious threat, so it seems ironic that he should stab Mercutio to death, treacherously it would seem, while he is being held "*under Romeo's arm*" (3.1.91 s.d.). Romeo is trying to prevent Mercutio from fighting.

Let us return again to the opening scene of the play, where the essential elements of the plot are introduced. There is a feeling of comedy in Romeo's love melancholy, his hopeless relation with Rosaline (whom we never see). Romeo's father speaks sympathetically about his stricken son, but also satirically, as do Benvolio, Mercutio, and all of Romeo's friends. It is unmanly to moon and pine in love. Romeo's speech is full of meaningless rhetorical flourishes, especially oxymorons, as he indulges himself in self-pity:

> O heavy lightness, serious vanity,
> Misshapen chaos of well-seeming forms,
> Feather of lead, bright smoke, cold fire, sick health,
> Still-waking sleep, that is not what it is!
> This love feel I, that feel no love in this.
> Dost thou not laugh? (1.1.181–86)

Of course, Benvolio laughs at this bombardment of words. How could he help himself? But Romeo continues with more oxymorons about love (1.1.193–97). His verbal display is unstoppable. Romeo is cured of his love melancholy when he falls in love with Juliet at the Capulet ball (in 1.5)— love at first sight, of course, which is a comic convention.

But in the scene just before Romeo meets Juliet (1.4), he is already full of a portentous sense of doom and disaster. This seems incongruous to me, as if Romeo is speaking for the play and not for himself. Romeo's speech comes right after Mercutio's splendid set-piece on Queen Mab. Benvolio is urging Romeo to make haste to the Capulet ball for fear of coming too late. Romeo is troubled by dire thoughts:

> I fear, too early; for my mind misgives
> Some consequence yet hanging in the stars
> Shall bitterly begin his fearful date
> With this night's revels and expire the term
> Of a despisèd life, closed in my breast,
> By some vile forfeit of untimely death. (1.4.106–11)

Again, there is a reference to the inauspicious stars we heard about in the Prologue ("star-crossed lovers"). The difficulty with Romeo's speech is that it has no relation to anything in the immediate context. Mercutio's dream of Queen Mab is positive and lyrical and has no forebodings in it. What fatal consequence hangs in the stars for Romeo? The play is clearly a tragedy, but it can't get to be a tragedy simply through tragic declarations.

There is another declaration of portents in Romeo and Juliet's wedding night, celebrated "*aloft*" (on the upper stage) in act 3, scene 5. Juliet is trying to persuade Romeo not to leave but Romeo insists he must speedily begin his banishment in Mantua. Juliet suddenly foresees evil:

> O God, I have an ill-divining soul!
> Methinks I see thee, now thou art so low,
> As one dead in the bottom of a tomb.
> Either my eyesight fails, or thou lookest pale. (3.5.54–57)

Romeo concurs in this bleak vision: "And trust me, love, in my eye so do you. / Dry sorrow drinks our blood. Adieu, adieu!" (3.5.58–59). Romeo exits with a polished couplet. But what is the nature of Juliet's sense of doom? It has no relation to its immediately joyful context of the wedding night, but it looks forward, proleptically, to the way the play will actually end in the Capulet monument. Like Romeo's earlier portent, it's as if Juliet is speaking for the play rather than for herself. Shakespeare seems to be exaggerating the need to reiterate that this is a "star-crossed" tragedy.

The role of Friar Lawrence in the play is ambiguous. When Romeo comes to visit him in his cell and asks to marry Juliet, the Friar's counsel is to go slow, and there is a sense in his advice that he is already predicting the tragic end of the lovers:

> These violent delights have violent ends
> And in their triumph die, like fire and powder,
> Which, as they kiss, consume. The sweetest honey
> Is loathsome in his own deliciousness
> And in the taste confounds the appetite.
> Therefore love moderately: long love doth so;
> Too swift arrives as tardy as too slow. (2.6.9–15)

The idea that Romeo and Juliet should "love moderately" goes against whatever we can gather about the nature of love, especially in Shakespeare's early comedies. The love-at-first-sight convention assumes that the lovers will be fully in love immediately. They don't start moderately and see their love grow, but they are at the climax presumably at first sight. That is why the Friar's idea seems so oddly out of place.

Friar Lawrence's scheme is to have Juliet drink a sleeping potion that will make her seem dead for forty-two hours, then awake in the Capulet burial vault and meet Romeo, who will take her to Mantua for their happy ending.

The plan is so elaborate and melodramatic that it seems unlikely to succeed in all of its particulars. Before Juliet drinks the potion, she has grave doubts about the Friar's motives. Her long soliloquy in act 4, scene 3 is important for our understanding of the Friar's role in this play. Juliet in her troubles has been more or less abandoned both by her mother and her Nurse. She knows that "My dismal scene I needs must act alone" (4.3.19). She fears that the potion will not work and provides a dagger with which to kill herself if need be. But, more importantly, she suspects the Friar of foul play:

> What if it be a poison which the friar
> Subtly hath minist'red to have me dead,
> Lest in this marriage he should be dishonored
> Because he married me before to Romeo?
> I fear it is; and yet methinks it should not,
> For he hath still been tried a holy man. (4.3.24–29)

Juliet is full of fears, but she takes the potion and is ready to try her fate. There is a maturity in Juliet that we haven't seen before.

One of the weakest touches in the plot is that Friar Lawrence's letter to Romeo in Mantua cannot be delivered because of a fear of infection. Friar John returns the letter, but Friar Lawrence is merely dismayed by the turn of events:

> Unhappy fortune! By my brotherhood,
> The letter was not nice [trivial], but full of charge,
> Of dear import; and the neglecting it
> May do much danger. (5.2.17–20)

Friar Lawrence doesn't have any Plan B ready for emergencies, but he proceeds to obtain an iron crowbar to go to the Capulet burial vault. His exclamation, "Unhappy fortune," fits only too well with the fatalism announced in the Prologue.

From the previous scene (5.1), we know that Romeo has heard of Juliet's death and burial. He resolves to buy poison from an impoverished apothecary and commit suicide by Juliet's side. The Apothecary, whom Romeo has lately seen "Culling of simples" (5.1.40), strangely resembles Friar Lawrence, whom we first see gathering "baleful weeds and precious-juicèd flowers" (2.3.8). Romeo, determined to take his own life, exclaims against astrological determinism: "Then I defy you, stars!" (5.1.24). This defiance is repeated in the final scene of the play (5.3) when Romeo drinks the poison:

> O, here
> Will I set up my everlasting rest
> And shake the yoke of inauspicious stars
> From this world-wearied flesh. (5.3.109–12)

But it turns out that whatever the "star-crossed" lovers do only enacts their preordained destinies.

*Romeo and Juliet* ends tragically as the Prologue predicted it would, but, at the end, there is still a sense that Romeo and Juliet are not tragic protagonists at all. As Capulet says to Montague, they are "Poor sacrifices of our enmity!" (5.3.305). Their deaths end the feud, but, when we consider the way the play moves, Romeo and Juliet remain innocents who, through no fault of their own, meet their doom. They can't be "Poor sacrifices of our enmity" and tragic at the same time. Shakespeare's tragic protagonists are always much more implicated in their destinies. They act, sometimes vigorously, on their own behalf. They are not just the sacrificial victims of fate.

*Chapter Eight*

# Audience Response to Richard in *Richard II*

There is a significant reversal in the audience response to Richard during the course of the play. We begin with a frivolous Richard stopping the combat between Bolingbroke and Mowbray, dunning the English public for his Irish wars, insulting the dying Gaunt, and disinheriting Gaunt's son, Bolingbroke. When Richard returns from the Irish wars, Bolingbroke has already invaded England. Although he invokes the divine right of kings, Richard is despondent and already prepares for his defeat and abdication. By the time of his murder in Pomfret Castle, he has become Christ-like in his sufferings and has fully won back the sympathies of the audience.

The opening conflict between Bolingbroke and Mowbray is puzzling, but it clearly has to do with the murder of Woodstock, Gaunt's brother and Richard's uncle. It is implied that Richard is involved in this murder, but it is never explicitly stated. Bolingbroke and Mowbray are ready for combat in act 1, scene 3, but Richard throws his warder, or truncheon, down and stops the fight. Why does the king allow the challenges in the first scene and the meeting of Mowbray and Bolingbroke in armor in act 1, scene 3 to proceed at such length? Is he so inordinately in love with pageantry for its own sake to allow events to go so far when he intends to break off the combat and sentence both Mowbray and Bolingbroke to exile?

By act 1, scene 4, Richard falls even further in the audience's esteem when we see him with his sycophantic minions, Bagot and Green, preparing for war in Ireland. Richard envies Bolingbroke's "courtship to the common people" (1.4.24) as if anticipating his ascent to the crown. Bolingbroke acts "As were our England in reversion his, / And he our subjects' next degree in hope" (1.4.35–36). Richard now does everything to alienate himself from the English commons by cruel exactions to pay for the Irish wars:

> And for our coffers with too great a court
> And liberal largess are grown somewhat light,
> We are enforced to farm [lease out] our royal realm,
> The revenue whereof shall furnish us
> For our affairs in hand. (1.4.43–47)

The "liberal largess" of Richard's court refers to the lavish expenditures that have almost bankrupted his "coffers." The "farming" of the realm was a much-hated practice by which, for ready cash, the king would sell to his favorites the right to collect royal taxes. Even worse, if the farming of the realm is insufficient:

> Our substitutes at home shall have blank charters;
> Whereto, when they shall know what men are rich,
> They shall subscribe them for large sums of gold,
> And send them after to supply our wants. (1.4.48–51)

"Blank charters" were deliberately left blank so that the king or his representatives could write in whatever sums they chose. The king's actions are not designed to win favor with either the commons or the wealthy.

At the end of this scene, when Richard hears of old Gaunt's grievous illness, he continues his reprehensible grasping for money to pay for his Irish wars:

> Now put it, God, in the physician's mind
> To help him to his grave immediately!
> The lining of his coffers shall make coats
> To deck our soldiers for these Irish wars. (1.4.59–62)

This anticipates the next scene in which Richard visits the dying Gaunt and not only insults him but also claims the estate that rightfully belongs to Gaunt's son, Bolingbroke.

In act 2, scene 1, the dying Gaunt delivers a blistering commentary on King Richard and the evils of his reign: "His rash fierce blaze of riot cannot last" (2.1.33). England " Is now leased out—I die pronouncing it— / Like to a tenement [land leased to tenant] or pelting [paltry] farm" (2.1.59–60). Here again is that unsavory word "farm" from the previous scene—and the "blank charters." England "is now bound in with shame, / With inky blots, and rotten parchment bonds" (2.1.63–64). It is at this point that the king enters.

York continues with his denunciation of Richard, pursued by flatterers and wasting the substance of once-glorious England: "Landlord of England art thou now, not king" (2.1.113). Richard cuts him off scornfully and calls him "A lunatic, lean-witted fool, / Presuming on an ague's privilege" (2.1.115–16). He spares his life because he is "brother to great Edward's son" (2.1.121), but he wishes fervently for his death. When Gaunt exits, Richard takes unlawful possession of his estate:

> And for these great affairs [the Irish war] do ask some charge,
> Towards our assistance we do seize to us
> The plate, coin, revenues, and movables
> Whereof our uncle Gaunt did stand possessed. (2.1.159–62)

This is exactly what Richard planned to do at the end of act 1, scene 4. York is scandalized because Gaunt's estate is the rightful property of his son, Bolingbroke, but Richard is determined to enrich himself to pay for his Irish wars: "Think what you will, we seize into our hands / His plate, his goods, his money, and his lands" (2.1.209–10). This is the lowest point in the play that Richard comes to in the audience's esteem. At the end of act 2, scene 4, Salisbury already predicts his downfall: "Ah, Richard! With the eyes of heavy mind / I see thy glory like a shooting star / Fall to the base earth from the firmament" (2.4.18–20).

When Richard returns from Ireland to face the army of Bolingbroke in act 3, scene 2, he is radically different. He now pursues an intensely lyrical melancholy that indicates that all is lost. His saluting the earth of England is a poetic and sentimental moment that marks the change in Richard:

> I weep for joy
> To stand upon my kingdom once again.
> Dear earth, I do salute thee with my hand,
> Though rebels wound thee with their horses' hoofs.
> As a long-parted mother with her child
> Plays fondly with her tears and smiles in meeting,
> So weeping, smiling, greet I thee, my earth,
> And do thee favors with my royal hands. (3.2.4–11)

Richard is fully aware that his personified invocation of Earth might seem foolish and misguided to his military followers: "Mock not my senseless conjuration, lords" (3.2.23), but he persists in his hopeless sense of the divine right of kings, that god will favor his cause:

> Not all the water in the rough rude sea
> Can wash the balm off from an anointed king;
> The breath of worldly men cannot depose
> The deputy elected by the Lord. (3.2.54–57)

At this point the audience cannot help sympathizing with Richard in his adversity. They are aided in their feeling by Richard's glorious poetizing.

Richard seems determined that he can make no effort to oppose Boling-broke. He wallows in his despair: "For God's sake let us sit upon the ground /

And tell sad stories of the death of kings" (3.2.155–56). Interestingly, he now seems to abandon the pomp and extravagance of kingship and to think of himself as a desperately needy man:

> For you have but mistook me all this while:
> I live with bread like you, feel want,
> Taste grief, need friends—subjected thus,
> How can you say to me, I am a king? (3.2.174–77)

This anticipates the shattering grief of King Lear on the heath.

Audience sympathy for Richard is promoted by the sorrow of other characters for the king, especially his queen. In the choral scene of act 3, scene 4, the queen expresses how forlorn she is made by Richard's fall:

> For if of joy, being altogether wanting,
> It doth remember me the more of sorrow;
> Or if of grief, being altogether had,
> It adds more sorrow to my want of joy. (3.4.13–16)

The gardener's report of Richard's plight is altogether desperate to the queen, who thinks in biblical imagery: "What Eve, what serpent hath suggested thee / To make a second fall of cursèd man?" (3.4.75–76). We are beginning to think of Richard's fall in religious terms.

The queen's grief is more fully developed when she meets Richard as prisoner on his way to the Tower:

> But soft, but see, or rather do not see
> My fair rose wither; yet look up, behold,
> That you in pity may dissolve to dew,
> And wash him fresh again with truelove tears. (5.1.7–10)

Richard is stoic in accepting his destiny, but he is unstinting in his poetic expression of sorrow. He tells his tearful queen:

> In winter's tedious nights sit by the fire
> With good old folks, and let them tell thee tales
> Of woeful ages long ago betid;
> And ere thou bid good night, to quite their griefs
> Tell thou the lamentable tale of me,
> And send the hearers weeping to their beds. (5.1.40–45)

Tears are the only recourse "For the deposing of a rightful king" (5.1.50). In their parting kiss, they are like the fated lovers in *Romeo and Juliet*. Richard says: "One kiss shall stop our mouths, and dumbly part: / Thus give I mine, and thus take I thy heart" (5.1.95–96). The tone is very different from the ranting Richard wishing Gaunt dead in act 2, scene 1.

Richard's final scene as a prisoner in Pomfret Castle shows us a transformed character. In his opening soliloquy, Richard is philosophical, comparing, with many biblical allusions, "This prison where I live unto the world" (5.5.2). He sees himself playing many different roles, ending with his death ("being nothing") (5.5.41). There is an important use of music in this scene (as there is in the statue scene [5.3] of *The Winter's Tale*). Richard's discourse on Time is also a confession of his misconduct, ending with a moving declaration:

> This music mads me: let it sound no more.
> For though it have holp madmen to their wits,
> In me it seems it will make wise men mad.
> Yet blessing on his heart that gives it me,
> For 'tis a sign of love; and love to Richard
> Is a strange brooch in this all-hating world. (5.5.61–66)

Love as a "strange brooch" is an odd metaphor, probably referring to the jewel worn in one's hat.

It is at this point, as though enacting an act of love, that a loyal groom of Richard's stable enters to declare his devotion to the king, a groom who "dressed" (5.5.80), or cared for, his "roan Barbary" (5.5.78) on which Bolingbroke later rode in triumph. Richard cannot resist a poetic comparison of himself and his faithless horse: "I was not made a horse, / And yet I bear a burden like an ass, / Spurred, galled, and tired by jauncing Bolingbroke" (5.5.92–94). Exton and the murderers soon enter and Richard is killed—after, however, he kills two of the murderers. It is interesting how thoroughly Richard is transformed in the audience's eyes from a frivolous, grasping, thoughtless person into a warm, suffering, Christ-like martyr.

## Chapter Nine

# The Fairy World of
# *A Midsummer Night's Dream*

It is important to remember that the fairies in *A Midsummer Night's Dream* are spirits and not mortals. This is also true of Ariel in *The Tempest*. The fairies are creatures of nature and are not restrained by the moral prohibitions of Christian society. Titania, for example, falls in love with Bottom disguised as an ass. As a spirit and not a mortal, she is uninhibited (as we see in many modern productions). The wood outside of Athens to which the lovers flee is symbolically a dark place, a place of night like Freud's Id, which the fairies rule. Magic is familiar in this world, and we should not be surprised that aphrodisiacs are so effective. The love juice is remarkably potent not only on Lysander but also on Titania, who can be made to fall in love with the next thing that she sees. In the world of the forest, love can be chemically induced.

We are introduced to Puck, Oberon's factotum, in act 2, scene 1. He is Robin Goodfellow or Hobgoblin, a mischievous spirit who delights in country tricks (but does no real evil). He is a "shrewd and knavish sprite" (2.1.33)

> That frights the maidens of the villagery,
> Skim milk, and sometimes labor in the quern [hand-mill for grain],
> And bootless make the breathless housewife churn,
> And sometimes make the drink to bear no barm [yeast, froth],
> Mislead night wanderers, laughing at their harm? (2.1.35–39)

He is Oberon's jester: he makes "him smile" (2.1.44) and performs tricks to entertain the Fairy King and his court.

Further in the play, it is obvious that Puck delights in petty knavery. He has put the love juice in the wrong lover's eyes. In his conversation with Oberon, he states his credo: "Lord, what fools these mortals be!" (3.2.115).

Mortals are inherently inferior to spirits like Puck and the fairy world, who are not foolish in love. Puck sees his function as a way to amuse himself:

> Then will two at once [Lysander and Demetrius] woo one [Helena];
> That must needs be sport alone;
> And those things do best please me
> That befall prepost'rously. (3.2.118–21)

Oberon is aware that Puck cannot be trusted, that thou "committ'st thy knaveries willfully" (3.2.346), and Puck seems to agree: "And so far am I glad it so did sort [fell out], / As this their jangling I esteem a sport" (3.2.352–53). Here again is Puck's word "sport" (which Iago also uses in *Othello*).

The quarrel between Oberon and Titania has important consequences for the material world, and especially for the weather and the seasons. As Titania informs us:

> Therefore the winds, piping to us in vain,
> As in revenge, have sucked up from the sea
> Contagious fogs; which, falling in the land,
> Hath every pelting [paltry] river made so proud,
> That they have overborne their continents.
> The ox hath therefore stretched his yoke in vain,
> The plowman lost his sweat, and the green corn
> Hath rotted ere his youth attained a beard. (2.1.88–95)

So the fairies can influence the processes of nature, so that everything is now topsy-turvy:

> The spring, the summer,
> The childing [fruitful] autumn, angry winter, change
> Their wonted liveries; and the mazèd [bewildered] world,
> By their increase, now knows not which is which. (2.1.111–14)

This testifies to the enormous power of the fairies over their natural domain.

When Puck puts an ass's head on Bottom, he is immediately transformed into an appropriate love object for Titania, which satisfies Oberon's revenge. As we expect, Titania's love is immediate and absolute, not depending on any physical or psychological factors. On waking, she declares at once: "What angel wakes me from my flow'ry bed?" (3.1.29–30). She is aware that Bottom is a mortal, but she promises to "purge thy mortal grossness so, / That thou shalt like an airy spirit go" (3.1.159–60). Bottom is unperturbed by this sudden passion: "reason and love keep little company together nowadays" (3.1.142–43). He accommodates himself to his new appearance as an ass with remarkable resilience. He only asks the fairies who attend on him for practical favors; for example, Mustardseed should help Cobweb to scratch him: "I must to the barber's, mounsieur; for methinks I am marvail's hairy about the face; and I am such a tender ass, if my hair do but tickle me, I must scratch" (4.1.24–27). There is no sense that Bottom expects Titania to keep her promise to make him an airy spirit. Even though he is disguised as an ass, Bottom has not changed at all from the old Bottom the weaver. He cannot return Titania's overwhelming passion, but he is always scrupulously polite and solicitous of her welfare.

At the end of the play, at midnight, the now married lovers all go to bed. Then, enter Puck with a broom, who speaks in rhyming tetrameters. The night is just the time for the fairies to emerge to bless the house and to bless the marriages. Puck speaks with solemnity:

> Not a mouse
> Shall disturb this hallowed house:
> I am sent, with broom, before,
> To sweep the dust behind the door. (5.1.386–89)

Then Oberon and Titania enter with all their train to continue the blessing of the house and the marriages. It all has a faintly religious tone. Oberon blesses the children that will be born from these marriages and promises that they shall be free of physical deformities:

> And the blots of nature's hand
> Shall not in their issue stand.
> Never mole, harelip, nor scar,
> Nor mark prodigious, such as are
> Despisèd in nativity,
> Shall upon their children be. (5.1.408–13)

Oberon speaks with authority, as if he can control nature.

The play ends with an epilogue by Puck, which is an interesting assertion of his importance. It is in his characteristic tetrameter couplets. He emphasizes the fact that it was all a dream:

> If we shadows have offended,
> Think but this, and all is mended:
> That you have but slumb'red here,
> While these visions did appear.
> And this weak and idle theme,
> No more yielding but a dream. (5.1.422–27)

In a gesture typical of epilogue speakers, he appeals to the audience for their applause.

*Chapter Ten*

# Shylock's Monomaniacal Style in *The Merchant of Venice*

The way Shylock speaks is unusual among Shakespeare's characters. He is perfectly fluent in his big speeches—for example, in the trial scene (4.1)—yet elsewhere he speaks with a monosyllabic, repetitive, broken syntax as if he were merely thinking about what to say. This is apparent in his first speeches in the play. In act 1, scene 3, his first five speeches merely echo Bassanio:

> Three thousand ducats—well. (1.3.1)
> For three months—well. (1.3.3)
> Antonio shall become bound—well. (1.3.6)
> Three thousand ducats for three months, and Antonio bound. (1.3.9–10)
> Antonio is a good man. (1.3.12)

So we are convinced that Shylock in his first five speeches has said nothing. The repetition of "well" suggests that he is merely thinking it over.

Suddenly, in his sixth speech, in his answer to Bassanio's question whether he has heard any imputation that Antonio is not a good man, Shylock launches into a formal, if not actually garrulous, reply: "Ho no, no, no, no! My meaning in saying he is a good man, is to have you understand me that he is sufficient" (1.3.15–17). This seems legalistic in its wordiness. Shylock even ventures a bad pun: "there be land rats and water rats, water thieves and land thieves—I mean pirates" (1.3.22–23). Now Shylock has become voluble. When Antonio enters, Shylock's aside is a perfectly fluent expression of his feelings: "I hate him for he is a Christian" (1.3.39) and "He lends out money gratis" (1.3.42). In justifying his taking of interest, Shylock goes to some length to cite the Old Testament story of Jacob and Laban and Jacob's trick to produce his share of parti-colored lambs.

Shylock seems to delight in the irony that his Christian enemy, Antonio, now comes to him to borrow three thousand ducats. With heavy sarcasm, he reminds Antonio of their previous relationship: "You call me misbeliever, cutthroat dog, / And spet upon my Jewish gaberdine, / And all for use of that which is mine own" (1.3.108–10). Shylock seems to be in his element in this long speech, which also seems to be colloquial in its easy mastery of speech rhythms:

> Well then, it now appears you need my help.
> Go to, then. You come to me and you say,
> "Shylock, we would have moneys"—you say so,
> You that did void your rheum upon my beard
> And foot me as you spurn a stranger cur
> Over your threshold! Moneys is your suit. (1.3.111–16)

Shylock is skillful in his mock quotations from Antonio, and he is conscious of his own act of speaking: "What should I say to you? Should I not say, / 'Hath a dog money? Is it possible / A cur can lend three thousand ducats?'" (1.3.116–19). Shylock also imagines other bitterly ironic roles for himself:

> Shall I bend low, and in a bondman's key,
> With bated breath, and whisp'ring humbleness,
> Say this:
> "Fair sir, you spet on me on Wednesday last,
> You spurned me such a day, another time
> You called me dog; and for these courtesies
> I'll lend you thus much moneys"? (1.3.120–26)

These speeches are histrionic. Perhaps that is what defines Shylock's mixed styles in this scene. He seems to be enjoying the confrontational roles he is playing.

Out of these speeches comes Shylock's seemingly sportive proposal of a merry bond without interest but only with the unlikely penalty of a pound of flesh on nonpayment. Shylock exults over his Christian enemies by emphasizing how harmless his merry bond is:

> If he should break his day, what should I gain
> By the exaction of the forfeiture?
> A pound of man's flesh taken from a man
> Is not so estimable, profitable neither,
> As flesh of muttons, beefs, or goats. (1.3.160–64)

Shylock wants to sound rational and practical: "To buy his favor I extend this friendship" (1.3.165). But we know that he imagines that it offers the promise of a bloody revenge on Antonio.

In act 2, scene 5, there is a peculiar disharmony in Shylock's speech. He begins by conversing with his servant Lancelot, who is leaving him and going to serve Bassanio, but his negative comments are interrupted by his calling for Jessica:

> Well, thou shalt see, thy eyes shall be thy judge,
> The difference of old Shylock and Bassanio.—
> What, Jessica!—Thou shalt not gormandize
> As thou hast done with me.—What, Jessica!—
> And sleep, and snore, and rend apparel out.—
> Why, Jessica, I say! (2.5.1–6)

Shylock's impatience with Jessica's delay in appearing is mixed with his contempt for Lancelot. His "conversation" with his daughter (she says practically nothing) is irritating because it is so broken. He is invited to supper, but he questions whether he should go: "I am not bid for love—they flatter me. / But yet I'll go in hate, to feed upon / The prodigal Christian" (2.5.13–15). In his cannibalistic image, he seems already to have acquired his pound of flesh.

Shylock is puritanical, and it seems to confirm that Shakespeare modeled his Jew on the many Puritans he knew in London. He frantically wants to protect his daughter, and his house too, from the music of the masques she might hear in the street:

> Lock up my doors; and when you hear the drum
> And the vile squealing of the wry-necked fife,
> Clamber not you up to the casements then,
> Nor thrust your head into the public street
> To gaze on Christian fools with varnished faces;
> But stop my house's ears—I mean my casements;
> Let not the sound of shallow fopp'ry enter
> My sober house. (2.5.29–36)

It is curious how strongly the "sober house" is personified.

This passage is more or less inverted in Lorenzo's magnificent speech on "the sweet power of music" in act 5, scene 1. Lorenzo could be speaking of Shylock when he says: "The man that hath no music in himself, / Nor is not moved with concord of sweet sounds, / Is fit for treasons, stratagems, and spoils" (5.1.83–85). This is an important and repeated idea in Shakespeare: villains are never lovers of music.

The flight of Jessica serves to accentuate Shylock's monomaniacal preoccupation with revenge. In act 3, scene 1, Shylock's reaction to Antonio's losses at sea is dire: "Let him look to his bond. He was wont to call me usurer. Let him look to his bond. He was wont to lend money for a Christian cursy. Let him look to his bond" (3.1.45–47). Shylock's repetitions are like those of the jealous Leontes in *The Winter's Tale* (especially in act 1, scene 2). They are a sign of an uncontrollable passion. His highly emotional oration, "Hath not a Jew eyes?" (3.1.56–57), is peculiarly mixed with the trivial and the portentous: "If you tickle us, do we not laugh? If you poison us, do we not die? And if you wrong us, shall we not revenge?" (3.1.62–64). It is hard to imagine anyone tickling Shylock or making him laugh.

In the trial scene (4.1), Shylock gives "humorous" answers to the Duke's request for mercy, but this is "humor" in the medieval, physiological sense of the four "humors" of the body, which are meant to be kept in the proper proportions for good health. Thus, when Shylock tells the Duke "it is my humor" (4.1.43), he means it is his whim, caprice, or fancy—not anything rational or normal. We remember that Ben Jonson wrote two plays based on the humors: *Everyman in His Humor* and *Everyman out of His Humor*. The examples Shylock gives for his deadly hate for Antonio are absurd and ridiculous in themselves: "What if my house be troubled with a rat, / And I be pleased to give ten thousand ducats / To have it baned? What, are you answered yet?" (4.1.44–46). Ten thousand ducats is an impossibly large sum to pay an exterminator—more than three times the value of the bond. Once begun, Shylock provides the Duke with even more extreme examples:

> Some men there are love not a gaping pig,
> Some that are mad if they behold a cat,
> And others, when the bagpipe sings i' th' nose,
> Cannot contain their urine; for affection,
> Master of passion, sways it to the mood
> Of what it likes or loathes. (4.1.47–52)

This is as close as Shylock ever comes to justifying his irrational impulses. The absurd examples culminate in his root principle: "Hates any man the thing he would not kill?" (4.1.67). The malice, previously concealed under various ironic changes of style, is now out in the open and plainly expressed.

## Chapter Eleven

# Commodity and the Bastard in *King John*

"Commodity" is a key word and key concept in *King John*, an early history play written after the *Henry VI* plays and *Richard III*. Its protagonist is not King John but Philip Faulconbridge, the bastard son of Richard, *Coeur de lion*, the brother of King John. In act 1, scene 1, the Bastard (as he is called in the play) readily accepts his illegitimacy rather than a rich inheritance from his supposed father, Robert Faulconbridge. King John calls the Bastard "A good blunt fellow" (1.1.71), like Kent in *King Lear*. He is a witty, straightforward, and aggressive speaker, and he bears a certain stylistic resemblance to Shakespeare's villains, especially to Edmund in *King Lear*, who also vaunts his bastardy. The king calls him a "madcap" (1.1.84), and he accepts his new status as knighted bastard with monosyllabic bravado:

> Something about, a little from the right,
> In at the window, or else o'er the hatch:
> Who dares not stir by day must walk by night,
> And have is have, however men do catch.
> Near or far off, well won is still well shot,
> And I am I, howe'er I was begot. (1.1.170–75)

These are all proverbial expressions about illegitimacy, but the Bastard glorifies in his status, which frees him from conventional morality.

His long soliloquy in the first scene establishes the important role he will play in the political action. He is a "mounting spirit":

> For he is but a bastard to the time
> That doth not smack of observation.
> And so am I, whether I smack or no:

51

And not alone in habit and device,
Exterior form, outward accoutrement,
But from the inward motion to deliver
Sweet, sweet, sweet poison for the age's tooth,
Which, though I will not practice to deceive,
Yet, to avoid deceit, I mean to learn;
For it shall strew the footsteps of my rising. (1.1.207–16)

This soliloquy sets forth the Bastard's determination to be a perfect courtier for the turbulent times in which he lives. He will be a cunning observer of everything about him, and he will not hesitate to flatter ("Sweet, sweet, sweet poison") when it is necessary.

His first triumph is to resolve the dilemma about the city of Angiers, which refuses to open its gates to either the English or the French. The Bastard has only contempt for Hubert and his followers:

By heaven, these scroyles of Angiers flout you, kings,
And stand securely on their battlements
As in a theater, whence they gape and point
At your industrious scenes and acts of death. (2.1.373–76)

"Scroyles" is a strong, slangy word used only this once by Shakespeare. The Bastard advises the French and English kings to join together to destroy "this contemptuous city" (2.1.384), then fight each other afterward. The Bastard is self-congratulatory about his ingenious plan: "How like you this wild counsel, mighty states? / Smacks it not something of the policy?" (2.1.395–96). "Policy" is a much used word of Polonius in *Hamlet* (and by many of Shakespeare's villains), referring to cunning statecraft in the style of Machiavelli.

The plain-speaking Bastard is clearly irritated by Hubert's high-flown, hyperbolical style:

He speaks plain cannon fire, and smoke, and bounce;
He gives the bastinado [cudgeling] with his tongue:
Our ears are cudgeled; not a word of his
But buffets better than a fist of France.
Zounds! I was never so bethumped with words
Since I first called my brother's father dad. (2.1.462–67)

The Bastard is being ironic here, since his brother's father is not really his own father.

His disgust with verbal affectation looks forward to Hamlet's reaction to Osric and especially to Laertes, who jumps into Ophelia's grave:

And if thou prate of mountains, let them throw
Millions of acres on us, till our ground,

Singeing his pate against the burning zone,
Make Ossa like a wart! Nay, an thou'lt mouth,
I'll rant as well as thou. (5.1.280–84)

The Bastard is uncomfortable with courtly rhetoric. "Bethumped" is again a colloquial word used only this one time by Shakespeare.

The Bastard is triumphant in act 2, scene 1, but the deal suggested by Hubert and agreed upon by the kings of France and England—to marry Lewis, the Dauphin of France, to Blanch of Spain, niece to King John—is abhorrent to him. He sees it as the way of the world, an easy but corrupt transaction, and this is the context for his important speech about commodity: "Mad world! Mad kings! Mad composition [compromise]!" (2.1.561). In order to persuade King John to this base deal, the King of France has whispered in the ear,

With that same purpose-changer, that sly devil,
That broker [pander] that still breaks the pate of faith,
That daily break-vow, he that wins of all,
Of kings, of beggars, old men, young men, maids,
Who, having no external thing to lose
But the word "maid," cheats the poor maid of that,
That smooth-faced [deceitful] gentleman, tickling [flattering] commodity,
Commodity, the bias of the world. (2.1.567–74)

"Commodity" is not used very often by Shakespeare in this sense, which includes in its meaning and connotations self-interest, gain, expediency, commercial advantage, and profit. The "bias of the world" is a bowling image referring to the weight on one side of the bowling ball, which causes it to swerve on an uneven course; in other words, the bias of the world refers to its crookedness. The Bastard expatiates on his master image of commodity:

The world, who of itself is peisèd [weighted] well,
Made to run even upon even ground,
Till this advantage, this vile drawing bias,
This sway of motion, this commodity,
Makes it take head [run] from all indifferency,
From all direction, purpose, course, intent.
And this same bias, this commodity,
This bawd, this broker, this all-changing word,
Clapped on the outward eye of fickle France,
Hath drawn him [King John] from his own determined aid,
From a resolved and honorable war,
To a most base and vile-concluded peace. (2.1.575–86)

Commodity is conveniently personified as a bawd, a broker, a pimp, who has a mellow and persuasive tongue. The Bastard ends his soliloquy with an ironic reversal:

> And why rail I on this commodity?
> But for because he hath not wooed me yet:
> Not that I have the power to clutch my hand [refuse the gift],
> When his fair angels would salute my palm,
> But for my hand, as unattempted yet,
> Like a poor beggar, raileth on the rich. (2.1.587–92)

The Bastard resolves upon an expedient course, in which he will respond to all the opportunities that offer themselves. He will be practical in leading England out of the dangers in which it is beset.

It is at this point that the Bastard takes over the leadership of England from King John. He flirts with commodity, as the inevitable way of the world, and concludes on an upbeat and positive note:

> Well, whiles I am a beggar, I will rail
> And say there is no sin but to be rich;
> And being rich, my virtue then shall be
> To say there is no vice but beggary.
> Since kings break faith upon commodity,
> Gain, be my lord, for I will worship thee! (2.1.593–98)

He now proclaims that he will use commodity for England's advantage.

It is interesting that, in *The Merchant of Venice*, Antonio uses "commodity" in a sense close to that of *King John*. The doomed Antonio understands that the duke cannot refuse to honor Shylock's bond:

> For the commodity that strangers [foreigners] have
> With us in Venice, if it be denied,
> Will much impeach the justice of the state,
> Since that the trade and profit of the city
> Consisteth of all nations. (3.3.27–31)

Venice as an international trading center depends upon the sanctity of its commercial agreements, its commodity. Without commodity, an important business word, Venice could not continue to exist. Like commodity in *King John*, it is "the bias of the world" (2.1.574), indicating the base and practical way the world must be run.

## Chapter Twelve

# Falstaff's Hyperbole in the *Henry IV* Plays

Falstaff is a creative and imaginative speaker. He is, by his own declaration (in *2 Henry IV*), "not only witty in myself, but the cause that wit is in other men" (1.2.9–10). As he says in this same passage: "The brain of this foolish compounded clay, man, is not able to invent anything that intends to laughter more than I invent or is invented on me" (1.2.7–9). Invention, or imagination, describes the ability of a poet or writer to find an appropriate subject matter. It would be going far to describe Falstaff as a poet, but he is excellent at using language creatively. I should like to talk about hyperbole in this chapter, which, like metaphor, offers a way of going beyond the literal meaning of words. In Falstaff's case, it may also be called exaggeration—or just plain lying—because hyperbole thrusts beyond ordinary usage.

To continue with this same passage, Falstaff expatiates on the young page that Prince Hal has sent him:

> Thou whoreson mandrake [a root shaped like a man], thou art fitter to be worn in my cap than to wait at my heels. I was never manned with an agate [a small figure carved in a jewel] till now, but I will inset you neither in gold nor silver, but in vile apparel, and send you back again to your master, for a jewel—the juvenal [juvenile], the Prince your master, whose chin is not yet fledge [feathered, covered with hair]. (1.2.14–20)

This is just a small sample of Falstaff's witty and complex style. He goes on with elaborate wordplay on the king's "face-royal," or ten shilling coin, which will never have any need for a barber, since it is the face affixed on an English coin.

Falstaff's hyperbolizing on the number of assailants he has faced in the robbery at Gadshill in *1 Henry IV* is an excellent example of his facility with words. His first enumeration is a large, rounded figure: "A hundred upon poor four of us!" (2.4.162–63). The number suddenly declines in his next speech:

> I am a rogue if I were not at half-sword with a dozen of them two hours together. I have scaped by miracle. I am eight times thrust through the doublet, four through the hose; my buckler cut through and through; my sword hacked like a handsaw—ecce signum! I never dealt better since I was a man. (2.4.165–71)

The numbers keep changing wildly. When Gadshill says "We four set upon some dozen—," Falstaff corrects him: "Sixteen at least, my lord" (2.4.175–76). The numbers expand as Falstaff expatiates on his heroic performance: "if I fought not with fifty of them, I am a bunch of radish! If there were not two or three and fifty upon poor old Jack, then am I no two-legged creature" (2.4.186–89).

What is interesting in this passage is how the numbers keep going up and down with unaccountable speed. When he is being more specific about the battle, Falstaff begins modestly by accounting for only "Four rogues in buckram" (2.4.197). But as the tale proceeds, the number grows:

*Prince.* What, four? Thou said'st but two even now.

*Falstaff.* Four, Hal. I told thee four.

*Poins.* Ay, ay, he said four.

*Falstaff.* These four came all afront and mainly thrust at me. I made no more ado but took all their seven points in my target, thus. (2.4.198–203)

Prince Hal and Poins egg Falstaff on in the practical joke, since they know that only the two of them set upon the fat knight. The number keeps increasing from nine to eleven, and the prince is suitably astounded: "O monstrous! Eleven buckram men grown out of two!" (2.4.220–21). When Falstaff is finally caught out in his exaggerations, he refuses to give any reasons for his tale: "If reasons were as plentiful as blackberries, I would give no man a reason upon compulsion, I" (2.4.240–42). Of course, there is a built-in pun on "reasons," pronounced like our "raisins."

Hal delivers a bunch of hyperboles about Falstaff's size: "this bed-presser, this horseback-breaker, this huge hill of flesh" (2.4.244–45), but the fat knight overtops him with hyperboles about Hal's meagerness:

'Sblood, you starveling, you eelskin, you dried neat's [ox's] tongue, you bull's pizzle [penis], you stockfish [dried cod]—O for breath to utter what is like thee!—you tailor's yard [yardstick], you sheath, you bowcase [holder for unstrung bows], you vile standing tuck [rapier]! (2.4.246–50)

The phallic imagery is evident here, including wordplay on "yard," meaning both "yardstick" and "penis." Falstaff always gives more than he gets verbally, and he is no match even for the clever Prince Hal.

When the two move into performances as the king and as Falstaff himself (and vice versa), Falstaff insists on outplaying and overreaching the Prince: "Give me a cup of sack to make my eyes look red, that it may be thought I have wept; for I must speak in passion, and I will do it in King Cambyses' vein" (2.4.387–90). He prepares for his role like a professional actor, parodying Thomas Preston's old play *King Cambyses* (1569) in the ranting style. This is like the readiness of Bottom in *A Midsummer Night's Dream* to take on the role of Pyramus in "Ercles' [Hercules] vein, a tyrant's vein" (1.2.41). Bottom boasts that he "could play Ercles' rarely, or a part to tear a cat in, to make all split" (1.2.30–31). Bottom and Falstaff are similar histrionically, but Falstaff is hardly naïve like Bottom. He is always self-conscious and purposive.

In his punning dialogue with the Lord Chief Justice in *1 Henry IV*, Falstaff insists on his youth, but the Lord Chief Justice strongly disagrees:

Do you set down your name in the scroll of youth, that are written down old with all the characters of age? Have you not a moist eye, a dry hand, a yellow cheek, a white beard, a decreasing leg, an increasing belly? Is not your voice broken, your wind short, your chin double, your wit single, and every part about you blasted with antiquity, and will you yet call yourself young? (1.2.180–87)

Falstaff answers with his own hyperbolical history:

My lord, I was born about three of the clock in the afternoon, with a white head and something a round belly. For my voice, I have lost it with hallowing [sanctifying] and singing of anthems. To approve my youth further, I will not. The truth is, I am only old in judgment and understanding; and he that will caper with me for a thousand marks, let him lend me the money, and have at him! (1.2.188–95)

Falstaff is not to be put down. His challenge to the Justice for a capering (dancing) contest is, of course, never to take place, but Falstaff is indomitable even in the face of supreme authority.

For a more extensive sample of Falstaff's hyperbolical wit, we have his long disquisition on his companion Bardolph's red face in *1 Henry IV*: "Thou art our admiral [flagship], thou bearest the lantern in the poop—but 'tis in the nose of thee: thou art the Knight of the Burning Lamp" (3.3.26–28). Falstaff plays on the romantic tale of Amadis, Knight of the Burning Sword, as will Beaumont and Fletcher later in their play *The Knight of the Burning Pestle*. But once Falstaff begins on his comic narration, he is not to be put down:

> I never see thy face but I think upon hellfire and Dives that lived in purple; for there he is in his robes, burning, burning. . . . O, thou art a perpetual triumph, an everlasting bonfire-light! Thou hast saved me a thousand marks in links and torches, walking with thee in the night betwixt tavern and tavern . . . I have maintained that salamander of yours with fire any time this two and thirty years. God reward me for it! (3.3.33–51)

Cold-blooded salamanders were supposed, in Pliny's natural history, to be able to live in fire. This long speech is spoken in grudging praise of Bardolph, although he doesn't seem to think so.

Like Shakespeare's fools, Falstaff has a number of set speeches on comic topics that are not necessarily related to the action in hand. I think the best of these is his long soliloquy on sherry in *2 Henry IV*. The speech is ostensibly addressed to Prince John of Lancaster, Hal's brother, a "sober-blooded boy" who "drinks no wine" (4.3.88–90). "Sherris-sack" is apostrophized as if it were an active force:

> A good sherris-sack hath a twofold operation in it. It ascends me into the brain, dries me there all the foolish and dull and cruddy vapors which environ it, makes it apprehensive, quick, forgetive [creative], full of nimble, fiery, and delectable shapes, which, delivered o'er to the voice, the tongue, which is the birth, becomes excellent wit. The second property of your excellent sherris is the warming of the blood, which, before cold and settled, left the liver white and pale, which is the badge of pusillanimity and cowardice. (4.3.96–106)

The upshot of the working of sherry may be seen in Lancaster's brother, Prince Hal:

> Hereof comes it that Prince Harry is valiant, for the cold blood he did naturally inherit of his father, he hath, like lean, sterile, and bare land, manured, husbanded, and tilled with excellent endeavor of drinking good and good store of fertile sherris, that he is become very hot and valiant. (4.3.117–23)

Falstaff functions as an entertainer, a performer, who contributes little to the historical action but is vital to the tone and mood of the play.

As a final example of Falstaff's hyperbolizing, we have his brilliant character sketch of Justice Shallow in *2 Henry IV*. It is also a long soliloquy spoken directly to the audience:

Lord, Lord, how subject we old men are to this vice of lying! This same starved justice hath done nothing but prate to me of the wildness of his youth and the feats he hath done about Turnbull Street [a disreputable London street], and every third word a lie, duer paid to the hearer than the Turk's tribute. I do remember him at Clement's Inn like a man made after supper of a cheese-paring. When 'a was naked, he was, for all the world, like a forked radish, with a head fantastically carved upon it with a knife. 'A was so forlorn that his dimensions to any thick sight were invisible. 'A was the very genius of famine, yet lecherous as a monkey, and the whores called him mandrake. (3.2.307–20)

Falstaff, the fat man, is carried away by the meagerness of Shallow: "you might have thrust him and all his apparel into an eelskin—the case of a treble hautboy [oboe] was a mansion for him, a court" (3.2.329–32). It is as if Falstaff, in hyperbolical fashion, wants to extract every last morsel of wit from his topic. It is interesting that he thinks that the subject of Justice Shallow will provide unlimited entertainment for Prince Hal: "I will devise matter enough out of this Shallow to keep Prince Harry in continual laughter the wearing out of six fashions, which is four terms [court sessions], or two actions [lawsuits], and 'a shall laugh without intervallums [intervals between terms]" (5.1.80–84). It is clear from this passage that Falstaff is always on the lookout for comic materials to amuse Prince Hal.

*Chapter Thirteen*

# The Banishment of Falstaff in the *Henry IV* Plays

It is clear that when Prince Hal becomes king, he will banish Falstaff. This is established in the first scene of *1 Henry IV* in which we see them together (1.2). It is a necessary fact of the plays that Prince Hal must banish Falstaff to become king. It is repeated over and over again that Prince Hal is only playing the scapegrace temporarily to establish his insight into ordinary English folk. The tavern in Eastcheap serves as an educational institution for Hal, but he is only following in his father's footsteps.

We remember what King Richard II in *Richard II* said about Hal's father, Bolingbroke, and his "courtship to the common people":

> How he did seem to dive into their hearts
> With humble and familiar courtesy,
> What reverence he did throw away on slaves,
> Wooing poor craftsmen with the craft of smiles . . .
> Off goes his bonnet to an oyster-wench;
> A brace of draymen bid God speed him well,
> And had the tribute of his supple knee. (1.4.24–33)

Bolingbroke becomes King Henry IV by deposing Richard and having him executed, but Richard could almost be talking about Prince Hal in this passage.

In act 1, scene 2 of *1 Henry IV*, Falstaff seems excessively concerned with what the Prince will do "when thou art a king" (1.2.23–24). This establishes a point of worry throughout these two plays. Hal participates in the robbery at Gadshill with his friend Poins as a kind of practical joke: "Well then, once in my days I'll be a madcap" (1.2.142). The stolen money is paid back afterward. The joke, of course, is on Falstaff. Hal's long soliloquy at the end of this scene is needed to establish the fact that he is playing the "madcap" for his own amusement and without incurring any harm to affairs of state. He is emphatic that he knows exactly what he is doing and that his association with low fellows like Falstaff and his crew is temporary: "I know you all, and will awhile uphold / The unyoked humor of your idleness" (1.2.192–93). "Idleness" is a strong word indicating foolery and foolishness.

Hal already anticipates the high style of kings when he speaks of himself as imitating the sun:

> Who doth permit the base contagious clouds
> To smother up his beauty from the world,
> That, when he please again to be himself,
> Being wanted, he may be more wond'red at
> By breaking through the foul and ugly mists
> Of vapors that did seem to strangle him. (1.2.195–200)

The reasoning in the soliloquy is logical, and it already anticipates an optimistic future:

> So when this loose behavior I throw off
> And pay the debt I never promisèd,
> By how much better than my word I am,
> By so much shall I falsify men's hopes. (1.2.205–8)

Hal is already determined on his future conduct, which will be brilliantly rewarded because it is unanticipated. The story of the Prodigal Son clearly lies behind this soliloquy.

Hal knows exactly how it will all end:

> And, like bright metal on a sullen ground,
> My reformation, glitt'ring o'er my fault,
> Shall show more goodly and attract more eyes
> Than that which hath no foil to set it off. (1.2.209–12)

His reformation is imagined as a jewel set off by the foil of his scapegrace days. The soliloquy ends with a resounding couplet: "I'll so offend to make offense a skill, / Redeeming time when men think least I will" (1.2.213–14). The idea that Hal has his redemption already in hand while he plays out his madcap days makes him seem like an awfully deliberate and purposive character. Redeeming time is an elaborate allusion to Ephesians 5:7, which refers to making amends for evil-doing.

Act 2, scene 4 of *1 Henry IV* goes over the same preoccupations as act 1, scene 2. Falstaff is still worried about being banished. When he plays the king in his mock-play with the prince, he praises himself as "A goodly portly man, i' faith, and a corpulent; of a cheerful look, a pleasing eye, and a most noble carriage" (2.4.427–29). He emphasizes the fact that "there is virtue in that Falstaff. Him keep with, the rest banish" (2.4.435–36). When Hal plays the king, he calls the fat knight "That villainous abominable misleader of youth, Falstaff, that old white-bearded Satan" (2.4.467–68). Falstaff defends himself, but there is an unusual pleading tone in his repetitions of the word "banish":

> No, my good lord: banish Peto, banish Bardolph, banish Poins; but for sweet Jack Falstaff, kind Jack Falstaff, true Jack Falstaff, valiant Jack Falstaff, and therefore more valiant being, as he is, old Jack Falstaff, banish not him thy Harry's company, banish not him thy Harry's company, banish plump Jack, and banish all the world! (2.4.479–85)

Prince Hal answers Falstaff's plaintive request with an ominous, monosyllabic declaration: "I do, I will" (2.4.486). Presumably, this seals Falstaff's fate because Hal is determined to banish him—he *will* banish him—as he has already more or less asserted in his soliloquy at the end of act 1, scene 2. Nothing has changed. In his conversation with the king, his father, in act 3, scene 2, Hal again declares his coming reformation: "I will redeem all this on Percy's [Hotspur's] head" (3.2.132).

The issues remain the same in the *2 Henry IV*. Hal's reformation is explicitly predicted by Warwick in act 4, scene 4. The ailing King Henry, who is near death at this point, grieves over his wastrel son: "Most subject is the fattest soil to weeds, / And he, the noble image of my youth, / Is overspread with them" (4.4.54–56). But Warwick is optimistic about Hal's coming change:

> The prince but studies his companions
> Like a strange tongue, wherein, to gain the language,
> 'Tis needful that the most immodest word
> Be looked upon and learned, which once attained,
> Your highness knows, comes to no further use
> But to be known and hated. So, like gross terms,
> The prince will in the perfectness of time
> Cast off his followers. (4.4.68–75)

Warwick is arguing, as Hal himself does, that the Eastcheap episodes are only an essential learning experience.

This theme reaches its climax in the next scene (4.5) after the prince has put on his father's crown, believing him to be already dead. In eloquent and moving speeches, he assures his father of his "noble change" (4.5.154) and convinces him of his sincerity:

> My gracious liege,

> You won it [the crown], wore it, kept it, gave it me.
> Then plain and right must my possession be,
> Which I with more than with a common pain
> 'Gainst all the world will rightfully maintain. (4.5.220–24)

Hal's ringing couplets effectively declare his commitment to being a strong and devoted king.

The scene with the Lord Chief Justice in 5.2, when Hal is already crowned as King Henry V, confirms Harry's moving reconciliation with his dying father in act 4, scene 5. He assures the Lord Chief Justice of his fealty:

> You shall be as a father to my youth.
> My voice shall sound as you do prompt mine ear,
> And I will stoop and humble my intents
> To your well-practiced wise directions. (5.2.118–21)

These speeches assure us of the rejection of Falstaff and his companions that follows in act 5, scene 5.

The king's speech echoes words he had used earlier; for example, "I know thee not, old man" (5.5.47) recalls his soliloquy at the end of act 1, scene 2 of *1 Henry IV*: "I know you all" (1.2.192) and Falstaff's frequent reiteration of his youthfulness. In *2 Henry IV*, King Henry V no longer has any use for Falstaff in his role as "a fool and jester" (5.5.48); he forbids him to reply "with a fool-born jest" (5.5.55). He now despises his idleness and fatness, and he deals with him as a bad dream from a long-forgotten time:

> So surfeit-swelled, so old, and so profane,
> But, being awaked, I do despise my dream.
> Make less thy body hence, and more thy grace.
> Leave gormandizing. Know the grave doth gape
> For thee thrice wider than for other men. (5.5.50–54)

It is odd to hear Hal using religious words like "profane" and "grace." He literally tries to redeem time: "Presume not that I am the thing I was, / For God doth know, so shall the world perceive, / That I have turned away my former self" (5.5.56–58).

So Hal presumes that he can affect his own transformation, his own redemption. There is a calculated purposiveness in all these assertions that does not make him into a warm and lovable character like Hotspur.

There is one further echo of Hal's former self in the opinions of the French in *Henry V*. The French ambassador who comes to the king to declare the Dauphin's defiance presents images of the madcap Hal that no longer apply to the heroic King Henry V: "There's naught in France / That can be with a nimble galliard won; / You cannot revel into dukedoms there" (1.2.251–53). Therefore, the Dauphin sends the king the insulting gift of a cask of tennis balls. King Henry issues his defiance of the foolish and misguided Dauphin, who "comes o'er us with our wilder days, / Not measuring what use we made of them" (1.2.267–68).

The Dauphin is still convinced that England is "idly kinged, / Her scepter so fantastically borne, / By a vain, giddy, shallow, humorous youth" (2.4.26–28). The Constable tries to persuade him that he is utterly mistaken:

> And you shall find his vanities forespent
> Were but the outside of the Roman Brutus,
> Covering discretion with a coat of folly;
> As gardeners do with ordure hide those roots
> That shall first spring and be most delicate. (2.4.36–40)

The message is enforced by Exeter, the English ambassador:

> And be assured, you'll find a difference,
> As we his subjects have in wonder found,
> Between the promise of his greener days
> And these he masters now. Now he weighs time
> Even to the utmost grain. (4.1.134–38)

This is the ultimate reiteration of Prince Hal's aim in *1 Henry IV* of "Redeeming time" (1.2.214).

# Chapter Fourteen

# Shakespeare's Illiterates

Illiteracy was common in early modern England. Perhaps half of Shakespeare's audience was not functionally literate (some might have been able to sign their name). Under the benefit of clergy rule in law, convicted felons would sometimes be freed if they could prove that they could read and write. In any case, I would like to look at several characters who are presumably illiterate. The most obvious is Dame Quickly in the *Henry IV* plays and *The Merry Wives of Windsor*. There is also the Nurse in *Romeo and Juliet*. The way they deal with the spoken language is purely phonetic. This is also true of the way Princess Katherine learns English in *Henry V*. Many of Shakespeare's servants and clowns are also illiterate, but I shall only speak about Dogberry in *Much Ado About Nothing*. The illiterate characters in Shakespeare not only stumble over words and their pronunciation; they also tend to be garrulous and circumlocutious.

Let us begin with Mistress Quickly in *The Merry Wives of Windsor*, particularly with William's Latin lesson administered by Parson Evans. Admittedly, we are dealing with Latin rather than English, but Mistress Quickly's responses are completely phonetic, without regard for how the language is written. The emphasis is on sexual meanings, since Mistress Quickly can only see inappropriately dirty words that she imagines the Welsh parson is teaching the naïve boy William. For example, when Evans asks William the word for "fair," he replies accurately "pulcher," but Mistress Quickly is scandalized: "Polecats! There are fairer things than polecats, sure" (4.1.26–27). "Polecat" is a word for a prostitute, as in Ford's exclamations against Falstaff, disguised as the witch of Brainford: "Out of my door, you witch, you rag, you baggage, you polecat, you rennion!" (4.2.178–80).

Evans's "focative case" is correctly glossed by William as "O—vocativo, O" (4.1.51), but Mistress Quickly hears the word as "fuckative," and "case"

67

is, of course, a word for the female genitalia. When the parson asks for the genitive case plural, William replies: "horum, harum, horum" (4.1.59), which puts Dame Quickly beside herself with indignation: "Vengeance of Jenny's case! Fie on her! Never name her, child, if she be a whore" (4.1.60–61). She is in a perfect tizzy about Parson Evans's instruction: "You do ill to teach the child such words. He teaches him to hick and to hack, which they'll do fast enough of themselves, and to call "horum." Fie upon you!" (4.1.63–66). The Latin declension "hic, haec, hoc" is endowed with sexual implications.

The language lesson in *Henry V* has a surprisingly close relation to the scene in *The Merry Wives of Windsor*. Princess Katherine is, of course, not an illiterate like Mistress Quickly, but she deals with her newly acquired words in English strictly phonetically, with a similar sexual misunderstanding. Her instructor is Alice, an old gentlewoman, who is not an expert in the English language. When she gets to the words for "le pied et le count"—the foot and the gown—she stumbles upon classic dirty words in French ("foutre" = fuck, and "con" = cunt).

Alice, of course, doesn't pronounce "count" as a native English speaker would, but she gives Katherine the phonetic cues she needs to fuel her indignation:

> Le foot and le count! O Seigneur Dieu! Ils sont les mots de son mauvais, corruptible, gros, et impudique, et non pour les dames d'honneur d'user: je ne voudrais prononcer ces mots devant les seigneurs de France pour tout le monde. Foh, le foot et le count. (3.4.49–55)

> (The foot and the count [gown]! O dear Lord! They are words that sound bad, wicked, gross, and indecent, and not for respectable ladies to use: I do not wish to pronounce these words before the gentlemen of France for all the world. Foh, the foot and the count).

Katherine is preparing for the wooing scene with King Harry, but it is already pervaded with the sense that English is a sexual language.

To return to Mistress Quickly, who has a prominent role in both parts of the *Henry IV* plays. In a scene with Falstaff in *1 Henry IV*, she mistakes in her anger a common English word:

*Falstaff.* Go to, you are a woman, go!

*Hostess.* Who, I? No; I defy thee! God's light, I was never called so in mine own house before!

*Falstaff.* Go to, I know you well enough.

*Hostess.* No, Sir John; you do not know me, Sir John. I know you, Sir John. You owe me money, Sir John, and now you pick a quarrel to beguile me of it. (3.3.65–71)

Mistress Quickly seems flustered by the English language, and she engages in endless repetition.

When she comes with officers to arrest Falstaff for debt in *2 Henry IV*, we see her, in her struggle with the right words, engaging in endless repetition and circumlocution:

> I pray you, since my exion is ent'red and my case so openly known to the world, let him be brought in to his answer. A hundred mark is a long one for a poor lone woman to bear, and I have borne, and borne, and borne, and have been fubbed off, and fubbed off, and fubbed off, from this day to that day, that it is a shame to be thought on. (2.1.28–35)

This is colloquial. She uses "exion" for "action" to indicate her pronunciation, "borne" and "fubbed off" are repeated to drive her point home, and "case" makes for a double entendre ("case" = "vagina").

In her next speech, Dame Quickly grows more impatient and unable to control her discourse:

> Throw me in the channel [gutter]! I'll throw thee in the channel. Wilt thou? Wilt thou? Thou bastardly rogue! Murder, murder! Ah, thou honeysuckle villain! Wilt thou kill God's officers and the king's? Ah, thou honeyseed rogue! Thou art a honeyseed, a man-queller, and a woman-queller. (2.1.47–52)

"Honeysuckle" and "honeyseed" are Mistress Quickly's endearing substitutions for the big, latinate word "homicidal," and the repetition of words in the whole speech indicates how disturbed she is. She seems hardly to know what she is saying because she is so confusedly devoted to Sir John Falstaff.

There are innumerable examples of Dame Quickly's vigorous and salty speech in this play, but I shall restrict myself to one further passage in act 2, scene 4. In the scene with Pistol, whom Dame Quickly calls "Captain Pizzle" (meaning the penis of an animal, such as a bull), he speaks in his characteristic mock-heroic style with bits and mangled pieces of classical and playhouse rodomontade. To indicate that he will not restrain his choler, he offers an heroic but essentially meaningless oration:

> Shall packhorses
> And hollow pampered jades of Asia,
> Which cannot go but thirty mile a day,
> Compare with Caesars, and with Cannibals,
> And Trojan Greeks? Nay, rather damn them with
> King Cerberus, and let the welkin roar.

Shall we fall foul for toys? (2.4.166–72)

Dame Quickly, who cannot understand a word of Pistol's speech, has, nevertheless, the perfect reply: "By my troth, captain, these are very bitter words" (2.4.173–74). Of course, there is nothing bitter about Pistol's nonsensical oration, but Dame Quickly catches the tone of it, and its seriousness and gravity are what she understands as "bitter words."

The Nurse in *Romeo and Juliet* is a character similarly conceived as Mistress Quickly in the *Henry IV* plays and *The Merry Wives of Windsor*. She is in the servant class, and she speaks with striking colloquialisms, notable errors in grammar and diction, and an expansiveness and repetition that verge on circumlocution. In her long, rambling speech in act 1, scene 3 establishing the age of Juliet, she wanders from topic to topic with great facility and wit:

> But, as I said,
> On Lammas Eve at night shall she be fourteen;
> That shall she, marry; I remember it well.
> 'Tis since the earthquake now eleven years;
> And she was weaned (I never shall forget it),
> Of all the days of the year, upon that day;
> For I had then laid wormwood to my dug,
> Sitting in the sun under the dovehouse wall.
> My lord and you were then at Mantua.
> Nay, I do bear a brain. (1.3.20–29)

There are many interruptions in the Nurse's speech as her mind wanders over her ostensible topic. There are also many repetitions and seemingly unnecessary specifications. Why does one need to know that she was "Sitting in the sun under the dovehouse wall"? What has the fact that "My lord and you were then at Mantua" got to do with Juliet's age? But the Nurse is proud of her strong memory ("Nay, I do bear a brain"), and she doesn't intend to spare us any detail that she can remember. There is, of course, no mention in the play that the Nurse is illiterate, but her speech (like Mistress Quickly's) suggests that she is speaking without any reference to English as it is written.

She also relates at great length and with suitable repetitions her husband's witty remarks at the time when Juliet fell down and cut her brow:

> And then my husband (God be with his soul!
> 'A was a merry man) took up the child.
> "Yea," quoth he, "dost thou fall upon thy face?
> Thou wilt fall backward when thou hast more wit;
> Wilt thou not, Jule?" and, by my holidam,
> The pretty wretch left crying and said, "Ay." (1.3.39–44)

"'A" is the colloquial contraction for "he." This is such a good joke that the Nurse repeats it twice in the next few lines.

The Nurse uses some odd colloquialisms; for example, when she is speaking to Romeo about Juliet after the ball, she assures him that "he that can lay hold of her / Shall have the chinks" (1.5.118–19). In other words, he shall have plenty of money. This is the only use of this odd word in Shakespeare, although "chink" figures importantly in Wall's part in the *Pyramus and Thisby* play-within-a-play in *A Midsummer Night's Dream* (5.1).

There is a similar vigorous slang in the Nurse's heated response to what she imagines as Mercutio's insults: "And 'a speak anything against me, I'll take him down, and 'a were lustier than he is, and twenty such Jacks; and if I cannot, I'll find those that shall. Scurvy knave! I am none of his flirt-gills; I am none of his skainsmates" (2.4.156–60). This is the only time that "flirt-gills" and "skainsmates" are used in Shakespeare (they therefore qualify as hapaxlegomena). There is still no adequate explanation of "skainsmates," although the Arden editor informs us that a "skain" was a long Irish knife. The Nurse also berates her servant, Peter, in terms with lively sexual innuendo: "And thou must stand by too, and suffer every knave to use me at his pleasure!" (2.4.160–61). Peter can only protest innocently: "I saw no man use you at his pleasure" (2.4.162).

The Nurse is best remembered for her tedious, teasing report to Juliet about her projected marriage to Romeo. The Nurse is exhausted from all of her running around on Juliet's behalf, but she can't seem to give the anxious Juliet a straight answer: "Your love says, like an honest gentleman, and a courteous, and a kind, and a handsome, and, I warrant, a virtuous—Where is your mother?" (2.5.56–58). Juliet is beside herself with anticipation; she obviously doesn't know how to deal with the Nurse's nonsequiturs:

> Where is my mother? Why, she is within.
> Where should she be? How oddly thou repliest!
> "Your love says, like an honest gentleman,
> 'Where is your mother?'" (2.5.59–62)

This makes for lively dialogue, but the Nurse, before she delivers her message, can only complain about her "aching bones" (2.5.64). The Nurse is well-meaning but practical. When she learns of Romeo's exile, she gives Juliet what she thinks is very good advice: "Your first [Romeo] is dead—or 'twere as good he were / As living here and you no use of him" (3.5.226–27). The vulgar "use of him" is not an expression Juliet would ever utter. She is obviously not in the same world of discourse as the Nurse, and she resolves "If all else fail, myself have power to die" (3.5.244).

I would like to look at one other character in Shakespeare, Constable Dogberry in *Much Ado About Nothing*, although there are many other servants and persons of the lower class who are equally ungrammatical and probably illiterate. In act 3, scene 3, Dogberry asks the First Watch: "who think you the most desartless man to be constable?" and he replies, "Hugh Oatcake, sir, or George Seacole, for they can write and read" (3.3.9–12). Presumably, Hugh Oatcake and George Seacole have unusual qualifications that are denied to Dogberry himself. He is an earnest speaker, but he has great difficulties with the English language, especially in the matter of diction. He often uses words that mean the opposite of what he thinks; for example, his "desartless" for "deserving." In act 3, scene 5, he has the memorable line "Comparisons are odorous" (3.5.16), which offers a wonderful alternative to the proverbial "comparisons are odious." Leonato's impatience with Dogberry and his companions is evident: "Neighbors, you are tedious" (3.5.18). The incomparable Dogberry, however, takes this as a compliment: "It pleases your worship to say so, but we are the poor Duke's officers; but truly, for mine own part, if I were as tedious as a king, I could find in my heart to bestow it all of your worship" (3.5.19–22). Why the "poor" duke? We will never find out. Leonato is astounded and doesn't know what to say to the innocent Dogberry: "All thy tediousness on me, ah?" (3.5.23).

Despite their difficulties with the English language, Dogberry and his companions manage to apprehend Don John's villains, Conrade and Borachio, although they don't know exactly what to do with them. Conrade has only contempt for Dogberry: "You are an ass, you are an ass" (4.2.74), but Dogberry has an invisible, linguistic protection against being offended: he takes Conrade's insult for a high compliment: "Dost thou not suspect my place? Dost thou not suspect my years? O that he were here to write me down an ass! But, masters, remember that I am an ass. Though it be not written down, yet forget not that I am an ass" (4.2.75–79). Dogberry's "suspect" for "respect" is what we have come to expect from him. Without his knowing it, he is a delightful and amusing speaker.

To conclude, when Don Pedro asks, in act 5, scene 1, "what offense have these men done?" Dogberry is only too ready to enumerate the case against them: "Marry, sir, they have committed false report; moreover, they have spoken untruths; secondarily, they are slanders; sixth and lastly, they have belied a lady; thirdly, they have verified unjust things; and to conclude, they are lying knaves" (5.1.213–17). All of which is true and spoken with notable vigor and colloquial energy.

## Chapter Fifteen

# The Wit Combat of Beatrice and Benedick in *Much Ado About Nothing*

The wit combat of Beatrice and Benedick in *Much Ado About Nothing* is a combat, a merry war, between two potential lovers. It is full of insults and provocations, and there is no certainty it will naturally end in marriage. One of the key questions of the play is whether Beatrice and Benedick need the plot of Don Pedro to make them fall in love or whether they will fall in love without interventions. It seems evident that the protagonists do indeed need artificial stimulation to bring them to marriage. They seem preoccupied with each other throughout the play, but that doesn't necessarily meant they are willing to surrender their aggressive, nonmarried state.

Beatrice's forthrightly independent—and harsh—tone is established in the first scene. In her first words in the play, she is already making fun of Benedick's martial valor. Speaking to her uncle, Leonato, she says: "I pray you, is Signior Mountanto returned from the wars or no?" (1.1.29–30). "Mountanto" is a fencing term for an upward thrust, and it implies that Benedick is a fencer rather than a soldier, but it also has an obviously phallic connotation. Beatrice continues with her comically contemptuous observations: "I pray you, how many hath he killed and eaten in these wars? But how many hath he killed? For indeed, I promised to eat all of his killing" (1.1.40–43). She cannot stop insulting Benedick's status as a warrior: "He is a very valiant trencherman; he hath an excellent stomach" (1.1.49–50). A "trencherman" is a gluttonous eater, hardly a heroic figure. Leonato feels the need to apologize for his niece: "There is a kind of merry war betwixt Signior Benedick and her. They never meet but there's a skirmish of wit between them" (1.1.59–61).

When Benedick appears in this scene, he continues the merry war with Beatrice, answering her in her own satirical language. When Beatrice says "I wonder that you will still be talking, Signior Benedick; nobody marks you," Benedick replies, "What, my dear Lady Disdain! Are you yet living?" (1.1.113–16). Benedick boasts that he is "loved of all ladies, only you excepted; and I would I could find in my heart that I had not a hard heart; for truly I love none" (1.1.122–24). Beatrice replies in kind, asserting her own independence from the attachments of love: "I thank God and my cold blood, I am of your humor for that. I had rather hear my dog bark at a crow than a man swear he loves me" (1.1.126–29). So it seems settled that the two radically independent spirits cannot possibly fall in love with each other.

At the end of act 2, scene 1, Don Pedro offers his ingenious plot to make Beatrice and Benedick fall in love with each other and marry: "I will in the interim undertake one of Hercules' labors, which is, to bring Signior Benedick and the Lady Beatrice into a mountain of affection th' one with th' other" (2.1.351–54). Don Pedro sees this as an almost impossible undertaking: "If we can do this, Cupid is no longer an archer; his glory shall be ours, for we are the only love-gods" (2.1.371–73). Leonato is skeptical: "If they were but a week married, they would talk themselves mad" (2.1.240–41), but he agrees to participate. Why is everyone so eager to marry off Benedick and Beatrice? There is a continuous theme in Shakespeare's comedies that the enemies of love cannot survive. Cupid is an all-powerful god who cannot be resisted. Besides, it seems incumbent on everyone in the play to create as many married couples as possible.

Benedick is the first one caught. In act 2, scene 3, he acknowledges his falling in love in a long soliloquy. He has pity on the imagined sufferings for love of Beatrice, and he yields immediately after the love plotters (Don Pedro, Claudio, and Leonato) have left the stage. He has no hesitation at all when he says: "Love me? Why, it must be requited" (2.3.219–20). He is determined to be "horribly in love with her" (2.3.230) and apologizes for his previous standoffishness:

> I may chance have some odd quirks and remnants of wit broken on me because I have railed so long against marriage; but doth not the appetite alter? A man loves the meat in his youth that he cannot endure in his age. Shall quips and sentences and these paper bullets of the brain awe a man from the career of his humor? No, the world must be peopled. When I said I would die a bachelor, I did not think I should live till I were married. (2.3.230–38)

It is a feeble excuse to attribute all to humor (whim and caprice), but Benedick is resolved to prove a lover. It is amusing that when Beatrice suddenly enters at the end of the scene, she obviously has no idea that Benedick is in love. He interprets everything she says as having a "double meaning" (2.3.252). He is intent on his new resolve: "If I do not take pity of her, I am a villain; if I do not love her, I am a Jew. I will go get her picture" (2.3.255–57). A Jew is meant as a person of no faith, and we remember how important it is for Portia's suitors in *The Merchant of Venice* to find her picture—"Fair Portia's counterfeit!" (3.2.115)—in the right casket.

The plotters—this time Hero and her two gentlewomen, Margaret and Ursula—are equally successful in getting Beatrice to fall in love with Benedick. She expresses herself, in soliloquy, in a measured ten-line sonnet at the end of the scene:

> And, Benedick, love on; I will requite thee,
> Taming my wild heart to thy loving hand.
> If thou dost love, my kindness shall incite thee
> To bind our loves up in a holy band;
> For others say thou dost deserve, and I
> Believe it better than reportingly. (3.1.111–16)

How can two such adamant enemies of love be won over so quickly? *Much Ado About Nothing* is clearly a comedy without a strong and intricate psychological underpinning.

Not to pause too long on the details of their love affair, by the end of the play Beatrice and Benedick seem to have returned to their normal, skeptical, witty selves. Benedick declares that he "was not born under a rhyming planet, nor I cannot woo in festival terms" (5.2.39–41). Beatrice coyly asks him, "for which of my good parts did you first suffer love for me?" (5.2.63–65), but Benedick is resolved not to be sentimental: "Suffer love! A good epithet. I do suffer love indeed, for I love thee against my will" (5.2.65–66). The conclusion is Benedick's: "Thou and I are too wise to woo peaceably" (5.2.71).

In the last scene of the play, the lovers return to their authentic mocking selves of act 1, scene 1. When Benedick asks "Do not you love me?" (5.4.74), Beatrice replies casually in the same terms: "Why, no; no more than reason" (5.4.74). When Beatrice asks Benedick the same question, "Do not you love me?" (5.4.77), he echoes her answer: "Troth, no; no more than reason" (5.4.77). We are meant to celebrate the fact that the lovers are once more witty speakers. They are not overwhelmed by love. When their companions inform them that they have each written love sonnets to each other, they are almost apologetic about them. Benedick says: "A miracle! Here's our own hands against our hearts. Come, I will have thee; but, by this light, I take thee for pity" (5.4.91–93). Beatrice replies in kind: "I would not deny you; but, by this good day, I yield upon great persuasion, and partly to save your life, for I was told you were in a consumption" (5.4.94–96).

Benedick's penultimate remark in the play ironically expresses his true sentiments. He urges Don Pedro to get married, with this moral caution:

"There is no staff more reverend than one tipped with horn" (5.4.123–24). The reference to "horn"—the horn of an animal—makes a familiar cuckoldry joke. Benedick takes pains not to be too solemn about the sacrament of marriage.

## Chapter Sixteen

# The Roman Style of
# *Julius Caesar*

*Julius Caesar* was probably written around 1599, at a time when Shakespeare was at the height of his powers. It is usually dated between *Henry V* and *Hamlet*. In style, however, *Julius Caesar* has no relation to those plays. It employs one of the smallest vocabularies of any play of Shakespeare, and it makes almost no use of figurative, lyric language. Its blank verse has a great many monosyllabic (or near monosyllabic) lines of nine or ten words, and it uses old-fashioned rhetorical devices like apostrophe that are associated with Shakespeare's earlier work, especially his poem *The Rape of Lucrece*. *Julius Caesar* is so unlike the plays of Shakespeare written around the same time that commentators have postulated that Shakespeare created a special Roman style for this play, one in keeping with its Roman subject matter.

Let us begin our discussion with Brutus's soliloquy. In act 2, scene 1, Brutus is meditating in his orchard, or garden, on what Cassius has told him in act 1, scene 2. He seems nearly convinced to join the conspiracy and to participate in Caesar's assassination. Never mind that Cassius's methods and some of his words are almost like those of Iago in *Othello*. His soliloquy at the end of this scene suggests a certain sleaziness in the way Cassius operates:

> Well, Brutus, thou art noble; yet I see
> Thy honorable mettle may be wrought
> From that it is disposed; therefore it is meet
> That noble minds keep ever with their likes;
> For who so firm that cannot be seduced? (1.2.306–10)

77

Obviously, Cassius does not consider himself "noble," as Brutus clearly is. He even says something mean-spirited (and echoed by Iago): "If I were Brutus now, and he were Cassius, / He should not humor me" (1.2.312–13). In other words, if the situation were reversed, Brutus could never hope to persuade Cassius to conspiracy.

Of course, Brutus doesn't realize that Cassius is seducing him. He cannot be aware that Cassius is throwing in at his windows fake testimonials from citizens attesting to the "great opinion / That Rome holds of his name" (1.2.316–17). The issue comes up again in the quarrel scene (4.3), where Cassius seems to be involved in taking bribes. Brutus is straight and direct, a perfect Roman in his strict morality, and his reasoning in the soliloquies in his garden is ethical and without any self-interest. He speaks to himself (and to the audience) with striking candor:

> It must be by his [Caesar's] death; and for my part,
> I know no personal cause to spurn at him,
> But for the general. He would be crowned.
> How that might change his nature, there's the question. (2.1.10–13)

The reasoning is, obviously, askew. Brutus rejects any personal cause, and this depersonalization is a distinctly Roman feature throughout the play. From the beginning, Brutus joins the conspiracy against Caesar for hypothetical reasons (very unlike Cassius's motives): "Then lest he may, prevent" (2.1.28). In other words, anticipate Caesar's proclivities (the old sense of "prevent") and kill him before he has the chance of becoming a tyrant.

In the first ten lines of this soliloquy, there are three monosyllabic lines with ten separate words: "It must be by his death; and for my part" (2.1.10), "It is the bright day that brings forth the adder" (2.1.14), and "And then I grant we put a sting in him" (2.1.16). There are also a couple of nine-word lines (11 and 17). This establishes a special Roman style throughout the play. It is serious and at times moving, but not particularly lyrical. There is an almost total absence of similes, metaphors, and figurative language. This is imagined to be the way Romans speak. Cassius is passionate and sometimes testy, but he also speaks in a Roman style, and this is also true of Caesar and Antony.

One rhetorical figure that is fairly frequent in the play is the apostrophe, or the address to a personified abstraction. This is typical of Shakespeare's earliest style. The use of apostrophes in *Julius Caesar* heightens the sense of formality and abstraction. Just before the conspirators enter, Brutus delivers in soliloquy an extended apostrophe to conspiracy, as if he needs to deal with the abstract idea of conspiracy, personified, before he can encounter the actual conspirators:

O conspiracy,
Sham'st thou to show thy dang'rous brow by night,
When evils are most free? O, then by day
Where wilt thou find a cavern dark enough
To mask thy monstrous visage? (2.1.77–81)

Brutus's "O's" are the sign that he is making an oration to conspiracy, as if it were an actual entity. He is more comfortable addressing "Conspiracy" than he is in talking with the conspirators. He answers his own question and gives advice to Conspiracy that is meant for the conspirators:

Seek none, conspiracy;
Hide it in smiles and affability:
For if thou path, thy native semblance on,
Not Erebus itself were dim enough
To hide thee from prevention. (2.1.81–85)

Brutus seems especially at ease stating his fears to Conspiracy personified. He is much better at making speeches than he is in dealing with persons.

Another apostrophe, to Error, is meant to account for Cassius's mistaken suicide. Messala speaks the apostrophe as if it should serve as a proper eulogy for the dead Cassius:

O hateful Error, Melancholy's child,
Why dost thou show to the apt thoughts of men
The things that are not? O Error, soon conceived,
Thou never com'st unto a happy birth,
But kill'st the mother that engend'red thee! (5.3.67–71)

The effect of the apostrophes is rhetorical. They are formal, they avoid the expression of personal emotion, and they are part of the general depersonalization of the Roman style.

If we turn to the orations of Brutus and Antony over the dead Caesar, we see that they fit well with what we have been saying about the Roman style. Brutus's speech is so formal that it seems to miss the mark as a heartfelt expression of sorrow. It is characterized by elaborate antitheses that seem intended to make rhetorical rather than personal points, and it is all spoken in a measured and balanced prose:

Had you rather Caesar were living, and die all slaves, than that Caesar were dead, to live all free men? As Caesar loved me, I weep for him; as he was fortunate, I rejoice at it; as he was valiant, I honor him; but, as he was ambitious, I slew him. There is tears, for his love; joy, for his fortune; honor, for his valor; and death, for his ambition. (3.2.22–29)

This is not a properly spoken style.

Brutus's rhetorical questions make for what we think of as an impersonal speech:

> Who is here so base, that would be a bondman? If any, speak; for him have I offended. Who is here so rude, that would not be a Roman? If any, speak; for him have I offended. Who is here so vile, that will not love his country? If any, speak; for him have I offended. I pause for a reply. (3.2.29–34)

Brutus's oration is essentially a political speech that contrasts what rude barbarians might think with the love of Romans for their country. Like Brutus's soliloquy in act 2, scene 1—"Then lest he [Caesar] may, prevent" (2.1.28)—the reasoning in the funeral oration is thoroughly specious. We are reminded that every decision Brutus makes in the play—not to kill Antony, to let him deliver a funeral oration, to fight the battle of Phillipi—turns out to be wrong.

Antony's funeral oration for the dead Caesar is very different from Brutus's, but it is also conceived in a recognizably Roman style. It imitates spoken discourse, as Antony says: "I am no orator, as Brutus is; / But (as you know me all) a plain blunt man" (3.2.217–18).

Antony's declaration anticipates what Iago will say in relation to Othello. Of course, Antony is not a "plain blunt man" at all, but he imitates one with great success. Notice how many monosyllabic lines there are in Antony's oration: nine- and ten-word lines. Antony forswears rhetoric in a style that is in itself highly calculated and rhetorical:

> For I have neither writ, nor words, nor worth,
> Action, nor utterance, nor the power of speech
> To stir men's blood; I only speak right on.
> I tell you that which you yourselves do know. (3.2.221–24)

Antony is cunningly denying the very purpose of his speech: "To stir men's blood," or to work up the mob's frenzied appetite for chaos and revenge. At the end, Antony denies responsibility for his speech's effect: "Now let it work: Mischief, thou art afoot, / Take thou what course thou wilt" 3.2.261–62). Incidentally, Antony is not above using a brief apostrophe to Mischief as a personified entity.

The upshot of Antony's oration is felt in the proscription scene, which is an epitome of the simple and direct Roman style, here seen as intensely impersonal, cruel, and political. The scene opens with a discussion of the enemies of the state on the list to die:

*Antony.* These many then shall die; their names are pricked.

*Octavius.* Your brother too must die; consent you, Lepidus?

*Lepidus,* I do consent—

*Octavius.* Prick him down, Antony.

*Lepidus.* Upon condition Publius shall not live,

Who is your sister's son, Mark Antony.

*Antony.* He shall not live; look, with a spot I damn him. (4.1.1–6)

The horror is that it is all so simple. Lives can be traded away with a mere checkmark on a list. It is in this scene, too, that Antony and Octavius agree to eliminate Lepidus, who is a mere "property" (4.1.40). It is all decided quickly and without emotion.

The most moving scene in the play is the quarrel scene (4.3) between Brutus and Cassius. This shows how effective the Roman style can be without any resort to figurative language or lyric outbursts. The previous scene prepares us for the quarrel. Cassius feels wronged by his "noble brother," that Brutus's "sober form . . . hides wrongs" (4.2.40), but Brutus is indomitable in his conviction of being morally right. So the quarrel begins with Brutus lording it over Cassius.

Brutus is trying to demonstrate what it means to be a true Roman, who participated in the murder of Caesar for ethical reasons:

> Remember March, the ides of March remember.
> Did not great Julius bleed for justice' sake?
> What villain touched his body, that did stab,
> And not for justice? What, shall one of us,
> That struck the foremost man of all this world
> But for supporting robbers, shall we now
> Contaminate our fingers with base bribes,
> And sell the might space of our large honors
> For so much trash as may be graspèd thus?
> I had rather be a dog, and bay the moon,
> Than such a Roman. (4.3.18–28)

Brutus is supercilious in his moral superiority to Cassius, who never denies any of Brutus's charges. Brutus freely condemns Cassius's "rash choler" (4.3.39), his "testy humor" (4.3.46), and his "waspish" (4.3.50) disposition, putting him on the defensive. Brutus can ignore Cassius's idle threats because he is "armed so strong in honesty / That they pass by me as the idle wind" (4.3.67–68).

There is a sharp break in the tone of the quarrel with the revelation that Brutus's wife, Portia, is dead:

*Cassius.* I did not think you could have been so angry.

*Brutus.* O Cassius, I am sick of many griefs.

*Cassius.* Of your philosophy you make no use,

If you give place to accidental evils.

*Brutus.* No man bears sorrow better. Portia is dead.

*Cassius.* Ha? Portia?

*Brutus.* She is dead. (4.3.140–46)

Brutus and Cassius are both represented as Stoics, who, it was popularly believed, were immune to the tribulations of fortune. Brutus steels himself, as we would expect from a proper Roman, from expressing his personal grief. The blank verse lines here tend to be monosyllabic. Brutus is a public figure, and there is no room for expressing private emotions, no matter how intense.

In the second announcement of Portia's death by Messala (which may well be a textual mistake), there is a similar Stoic and Roman impassivity:

*Brutus.* Now as you are a Roman, tell me true.

*Messala.* Then like a Roman bear the truth I tell.

For certain she is dead, and by strange manner.

*Brutus.* Why, farewell, Portia. We must die, Messala.

With meditating that she must die once,

I have the patience to endure it now. (4.3.184–89)

This is very like the first time that Brutus learns of his wife's death. "Why, farewell, Portia. We must die, Messala" is unlike Shakespeare's long and eloquent death speeches (as in *Hamlet*), but it is moving in its simplicity and Stoic spareness.

One other notable aspect of the quarrel scene is the entrance of an un-named poet, who seeks to reconcile Brutus and Cassius. But they both find the poet equally unwelcome. Cassius says: "Ha, ha! How vilely doth this cynic rhyme!" (4.3.130), although we don't hear the poet say anything once he has appeared. Brutus is more emphatic in his rejection: "What should the wars do with these jigging fools?" (4.3.134). This is a comment not only on the poet but also on the Roman style, which has nothing to do with "jigging" speech. This is like the treatment of Cinna the Poet in act 3, scene 3, which immediately follows Antony's funeral oration. It is useless for Cinna to protest that he is Cinna the Poet and not Cinna the Conspirator. The uncontrollable plebeian mob, fresh from Antony's oration, are out for blood— "Tear him for his bad verses! Tear him for his bad verses!" (3.3.32–33)—and further: "It is no matter, his name's Cinna; pluck but his name out of his heart, and turn him going" (3.3.35–37). This is frighteningly political, as is the proscription scene (4.1) that follows. The Roman style is meant to accommodate itself to the harsh realities of the Roman world.

# Chapter Seventeen

# Jaques as Satiric Observer in *As You Like It*

Shakespeare has a number of characters who function as satiric observers and commentators in their plays: Lucio in *Measure for Measure*, Thersites in *Troilus and Cressida*, and Apemantus in *Timon of Athens*. These are not particularly attractive characters, but they serve as truth-speakers in their respective plays. Jaques is like Touchstone, the clown, in satirizing artificial pastoral conventions and romantic affirmations. They are clearly not like the exiled Duke Senior, who speaks so positively of his pastoral existence in the Forest of Arden:

> Sweet are the uses of adversity,
> Which, like the toad, ugly and venomous,
> Wears yet a precious jewel in his head;
> And this our life, exempt from public haunt,
> Finds tongues in trees, books in the running brooks,
> Sermons in stones, and good in everything. (2.1.12–17)

Jaques is a malcontent, a figure out of the violent satiric poetry of the 1590s, which the Bishops decided to forbid. Orlando bids him farewell as "good Monsieur Melancholy" (3.2.294–95), and act 4, scene 1 opens with an extended dialogue between Jaques and Rosalind in which he acknowledges that "'tis good to be sad and say nothing" (4.1). He seems proud of his own unique melancholy, which is unlike that of the scholar, the musician, the courtier, the soldier, the lady, or the lover: "it is a melancholy of mine own, compounded of many simples, extracted from many objects, and indeed the sundry contemplation of my travels, in which my often rumination wraps me in a most humorous sadness" (4.1.15–19). His "sadness" is "humorous" in the sense that it is composed primarily of an effusion of black bile. At the end of the play, Jaques decides to remain in the Forest of Arden because "There is much matter to be heard and learned" from these "convertites" (5.4.185). Presumably he is referring to Duke Frederick, who "hath put on a religious life / And thrown into neglect the pompous court" (5.4.181–82).

The name Jaques is pronounced "Jakes," the word for a toilet, although it may also be pronounced with a light second syllable ("Jak-is"). "Qu" is always pronounced like a "k" in Elizabethan English. Sir John Harington, the translator of Ariosto, wrote an amusing little book called *The Metamorphosis of Ajax* in 1596, which is a mock-heroic account, with illustrations, of the early invention of the toilet (Ajax = a jakes). That is apparently why Touchstone doesn't call Jaques by his proper name but addresses him as "good Master What-ye-call't" (3.3.72–73). All of these indications establish Jaques as a comic character, a kind of entertainer of the exiled court. Duke Senior seeks him out, as he might seek out the fool, and asserts: "I love to cope him in these sullen fits, / For then he's full of matter" (2.1.67–68).

There is a certain absurdity when we first encounter Jaques and hear about his "weeping and commenting / Upon the sobbing deer" (2.1.65–66). He "moralizes" upon the deer in a manner that parodies sentimental effusions. For example, when the "careless herd" of deer pass by the wounded deer without pausing to greet him, Jaques the moralist interprets this in human terms:

> "Ay," quoth Jaques,
> "Sweep on, you fat and greasy citizens,
> 'Tis just the fashion: wherefore do you look
> Upon that poor and broken bankrupt there?" (2.1.54–57)

The sentimentality of Jaques's anthropomorphic views is what Duke Senior and his court find so entertaining. As the First Lord observes with amusement:

> Thus most invectively he pierceth through
> The body of the country, city, court,
> Yea, and of this our life, swearing that we
> Are mere usurpers, tyrants, and what's worse,
> To fright the animals and to kill them up
> In their assigned and native dwelling place. (2.1.58–63)

Jaques is enamored with Touchstone, the fool, and he insists that he have the fool's allowed privilege of playing the role of the satirist:

> I must have liberty
> Withal, as large a charter as the wind,
> To blow on whom I please, for so fools have.

And they that are most gallèd with my folly,
They most must laugh. (2.7.47–51)

Touchstone says nothing in the play about the fool's therapeutic social role, but Jaques is voluble about what it means to be a fool:

Invest me in my motley, give me leave
To speak my mind, and I will through and through
Cleanse the foul body of th' infected world,
If they will patiently receive my medicine. (2.7.58–61)

But why should the world be so receptive to Jaques?

Duke Senior doesn't take Jaques seriously as a moral satirist, and he usefully reminds us of Jaques's history:

Most mischievous foul sin, in chiding sin.
For thou thyself hast been a libertine,
As sensual as the brutish sting itself;
And all th' embossèd sores and headed evils
That thou with license of free foot hast caught,
Wouldst thou disgorge into the general world. (2.7.64–69)

This is a valuable undercutting of Jaques shortly before he delivers his famous speech on the seven ages of man.

Granted that "All the world's a stage" (2.7.138), but Jaques is cynical and sour about man's life. Every stage is represented satirically, beginning with the infant "Mewling [bawling] and puking in the nurse's arms" (2.7.143). In a play devoted to the seriousness of love, Jaques disparages the lover: "Sighing like furnace, with a woeful ballad / Made to his mistress' eyebrow" (2.7.147–48). The last age, "That ends this strange eventful history, / Is second childishness and mere [utter] oblivion, / Sans teeth, sans eyes, sans taste, sans everything" (2.7.163–65). Despite the fact that this speech is usually quoted as an example of Shakespeare's cynical profundity, in Jaques's mouth it is a shallow and laughable set piece.

The last line of the speech is a good example of Jaques's affected speech. We know from *Love's Labor's Lost* that "sans" is a precious sounding gallicism. In pleading for his sincerity in wanting to be married, Berowne says: "My love to thee is sound, sans crack or flaw," but Rosaline will have none of his posturing: "Sans 'sans,' I pray you" (5.2.416–17). Another notable example is in Jaques's parody song in act 2, scene 5:

If it do come to pass
That any man turn ass,
Leaving his wealth and ease
A stubborn will to please,

Ducdame, ducdame, ducdame.
Here shall he see gross fools as he,
An if he will come to me. (2.5.46–51)

Amiens doesn't understand: "What's that 'ducdame'"?, but Jaques says only
"'Tis a Greek invocation to call fools into a circle" (2.5.55–56). Is "ducdame" nonsensical doubletalk, as Feste speaks in *Twelfth Night*? The whole
poem is, in fact, doggerel nonsense.

In the same scene, Jaques asks Amiens to continue singing: "Come, more,
another stanzo! Call you 'em stanzos?" (2.5.17–18). "Stanzo" is an affected
Italianism for the plain English word "stanza." So it goes. Jaques, a follower
of the exiled Duke Senior, makes himself indispensable in *As You Like It*. We
feel as if the role of Touchstone as fool is doubled, since Jaques is devoted to
Touchstone and wants to be invested in his motley cloak. If Jaques cannot be
the fool proper, he is nevertheless a highly original, satirical commentator on
the action.

## Chapter Eighteen

# Feste as Corrupter of Words
# in *Twelfth Night*

When Viola asks Feste the clown if he is Lady Olivia's fool, he vigorously denies the name:

> No, indeed, sir. The Lady Olivia has no folly. She will keep no fool, sir, till she be married; and fools are as like husbands as pilchers [small herrings] are to herrings—the husband's the bigger. I am indeed not her fool, but her corrupter of words. (3.1.33–37)

Feste's verbal dexterity is astounding, and he ranges from double-talk and learned nonsense to outright parody, to puns and wordplay, and to acting many roles, including Sir Topas the curate, who comes to cure the "mad" Malvolio. Feste is conscious of words in and for themselves and their fashionable usage. For example, his answer to Viola in 3.1 makes fun not only of the archaic term "welkin" for sky but also of the newfangled word "element": "Who you are and what you would are out of my welkin; I might say 'element,' but the word is overworn" (3.1.58–60). We remember that Malvolio uses the pretentious word "element" a bit further on in act 3: "You are idle shallow things; I am not of your element" (3.4.127–28). The foolish Sir Andrew is busy writing down Feste's remarkable lexicon in his notebook. He is Feste's inordinate admirer (as is Jaques with Touchstone in *As You Like It*). Sir Andrew remembers exactly what Feste said the evening before: "In sooth, thou wast in very gracious fooling last night, when thou spok'st of Pigrogromitus, of the Vapians passing the equinoctial of Queubus" (2.3.21–24).

Commentators have puzzled over what Feste could possibly mean, but it is all probably his own mock-learning, expressed in parodic double-talk. His reply to Sir Andrew continues the satirical language coining of his last night's performance: "I did impeticos thy gratillity, for Malvolio's nose is no whipstock. My lady has a white hand, and the Myrmidons are no bottle-ale houses" (2.3.26–28). This is more or less comprehensible—"gratillity" is Feste's coinage for "gratuity"—but the naïve Sir Andrew is duly impressed by these language games.

There is another good example of Feste's verbal facility when he is talking with Olivia in act 1, scene 5: "Wit, and't be thy will, put me into good fooling. Those wits that think they have thee do very often prove fools, and I that am sure I lack thee may pass for a wise man. For what says Quinapalus? 'Better a witty fool than a foolish wit'" (1.5.33–37). Quinapalus is an invented Latin authority, probably related to Quintilian, the writer on rhetoric. The clown delights in quoting from nonexistent texts, and he is, at best, a tricky speaker, pursuing his own themes at the expense of his listeners.

These mock-quotations reach their apex when Feste is preparing to play Sir Topas, the curate, who is ministering to the mad Malvolio. He demonstrates his histrionic skill for the admiring Sir Toby: "Bonos dies, Sir Toby; for, as the old hermit of Prague, that never saw pen and ink, very wittily said to a niece of King Gorboduc, 'That that is is'; so, I, being Master Parson, am Master Parson; for what is 'that' but that, and 'is' but is?" (4.2.13–17). Feste has bits and pieces of learning, like Pistol in *2 Henry IV*. He also parodies scholastic debates about the meaning of relatively meaningless words. Sir Toby is duly impressed with Feste's performance: "The knave counterfeits well; a good knave" (4.2.20).

Feste is nothing short of brilliant in the role of Sir Topas. Malvolio is convinced that he is dealing with a learned clergyman who will help him prove that he is not mad. Sir Topas speaks in mock-theological style, imitating the close analytic reasoning of scholastic texts. Feste disputes Malvolio's assertion that "They have laid me here in hideous darkness" (4.2.30–31): no, the house "hath bay windows transparent as barricadoes, and the clerestories toward the north south are as lustrous as ebony; and yet complainest thou of obstruction?" (4.2.37–40). Of course, there is no such direction as "south north"; ebony is a type image of intense blackness; and barricadoes are impenetrably dark. Malvolio, however, is duly impressed with the quality of Sir Topas's reasoning.

Feste caps his examination of Malvolio's madness with a mock-catechism that draws on Pythagorean metempsychosis:

*Clown.* What is the opinion of Pythagoras concerning wild fowl?

*Malvolio.* That the soul of our grandam might happily inhabit a bird.

*Clown.* What think'st thou of his opinion?

*Malvolio.* I think nobly of the soul and no way approve his opinion.

*Clown.* Fare thee well. Remain thou still in darkness. Thou shalt hold th' opinion of Pythagoras ere I will allow of thy wits, and fear to kill a woodcock, lest thou dispossess the soul of thy grandam. (4.2.50–60)

Feste's joke is lost on Malvolio, who plays the straight man and answers as if Pythagoras were indeed an important Christian theologian. The Clown continues his jesting about Malvolio when he reads his letter to Olivia in an exceptionally loud voice. Olivia is startled: "How now? Art thou mad?" (5.1.294), but Feste justifies himself literally: "No, madam, I do but read madness. And your ladyship will have it as it ought to be, you must allow *vox*" (5.1.295–97). "Vox" signifies the appropriate voice of a madman.

Thus Feste entertains us throughout the play. He attacks foolishness of all sorts, especially verbal, and he parodies pretentious learning as often as he can. He indulges in wordplay and language games, so that no one can anticipate what he will actually say. For example, in act 1, scene 5, Maria upbraids him: "Yet you will be hanged for being so long absent, or be turned away. Is not that as good as a hanging to you?" (1.5.16–18). But the Clown has a ready answer: "Many a good hanging prevents a bad marriage, and for turning away, let summer bear it out" (1.5.19–21). This is either a proverb or a mock-proverb, and the Arden editor sees a sexual connotation in being well hung. For turning away, summer is good weather for being without an occupation.

At the end of the play, the clown's song about the seven ages of man is bitter-sweet and functions as a kind of epilogue:

> When that I was and a little tiny boy,
> With hey, ho, the wind and the rain,
> A foolish thing was but a toy [trifle],
> For the rain it raineth every day. (5.1.390–93)

The Fool in *King Lear* sings a stanza of what seems like an adaptation of Feste's song (3.2.74–77). Feste's last stanza functions like an epilogue to the play:

> A great while ago the world begun,
> Hey, ho, the wind and the rain;
> But that's all one, our play is done,
> And we'll strive to please you every day. (5.1.406–9)

It is some clue to Feste's significance as a character in *Twelfth Night* that he sings the last words of the play. He is very important for establishing the tone of the play.

## Chapter Nineteen

# Hamlet as Actor

It's surprising how strong an emphasis there is in *Hamlet* on the protagonist as an actor who is closely connected with the theater. This is one of the dominant imageries in the play. In Hamlet's first scene in the court of Denmark, the prince answers his mother's facile attempt to cure him of his melancholy: "Why seems it so particular with thee?" (1.2.75). Hamlet speaks of his mourning dress as if it were an actor's costume in which he can play the appropriate role of grieving son:

> Seems, madam? Nay, it is. I know not "seems."
> 'Tis not alone my inky cloak, good mother,
> Nor customary suits of solemn black,
> Nor windy suspiration of forced breath,
> No, nor the fruitful river in the eye,
> Nor the dejected havior of the visage,
> Together with all forms, moods, shapes of grief,
> That can denote me truly. (1.2.76–83)

Hamlet makes an important contrast between his inner and real grief at the death of his father and its external signs:

> These indeed seem,
> For they are actions that a man might play,
> But I have that within which passes show;
> These but the trappings and the suits of woe. (1.2.83–86)

Hamlet the actor is insisting that he is not merely acting the part of mourning son, but that he feels it deeply within. This sets up a contrast between inner and outer realities that continues throughout the play.

Hamlet is acutely conscious of his own style, which we can see very well in the soliloquy at the end of act 2, after he has met with the players. He is impressed with the fact that the Player, in speaking of Hecuba, can get so personally involved "But in a fiction, in a dream of passion" (2.2.562). The basic paradox is: "What's Hecuba to him, or he to Hecuba, / That he should weep for her?" (2.2.564–65). This gets to the heart of what acting means. Hamlet's question is all about the contrast of the inner and the outer reality: "What would he do / Had he the motive and the cue for passion / That I have?" (2.2.565–67). Hamlet then proceeds, like an actor, to work himself up to a grand passion:

> Who calls me villain? Breaks my pate across?
> Plucks off my beard and blows it in my face?
> Tweaks me by the nose? Gives me the lie i' th' throat
> As deep as to the lungs? Who does me this?
> Ha, 'swounds, I should take it, for it cannot be
> But I am pigeon-livered and lack gall
> To make oppression bitter, or ere this
> I should ha' fatted all the region kites
> With this slave's offal. Bloody, bawdy villain!
> Remorseless, treacherous, lecherous, kindless villain!
> O, vengeance! (2.2.583–93)

This is like Bottom the weaver in *A Midsummer Night's Dream* preparing to play the role of Pyramus, which he imagines as "a part to tear a cat in, to make all split" (1.2.30–31).

Hamlet is conscious of the fact that he is ranting like a bad actor, and he suddenly breaks off:

> Why, what an ass am I! This is most brave,
> That I, the son of a dear father murdered,
> Prompted to my revenge by heaven and hell,
> Must, like a whore, unpack my heart with words
> And fall a-cursing like a very drab,
> A stallion! Fie upon't, foh! (2.2.594–99)

"Brave" is used as a negative word, implying bravado and showing off. Hamlet is aware of doing exactly what he warned the players against at the beginning of act 3, scene 2, of tearing "a passion to tatters, to very rags, to split the ears of the groundlings" (3.2.10–11). This is the kind of acting that "out-herods Herod" (3.2.14).

There is another scene, at Ophelia's grave, that echoes the style of Hamlet's soliloquy at the end of act 2, scene 2. Hamlet parodies the aggrieved Laertes's overblown speech when he has leaped into Ophelia's newly made grave:

What is he whose grief
Bears such an emphasis, whose phrase of sorrow
Conjures the wand'ring stars, and makes them stand
Like wonder-wounded hearers? (5.1.254–57)

After Hamlet and Laertes "grapple," Hamlet goes even further in parodying Laertes's exaggerated rhetoric:

Dost thou come here to whine?
To outface me with leaping in her grave?
Be buried quick with her, and so will I.
And if thou prate of mountains, let them throw
Millions of acres on us, till our ground,
Singeing his pate against the burning zone,
Make Ossa like a wart! (5.1.277–83)

Remember how contemptuously Hamlet spoke about the dead Polonius: "Indeed, this counselor / Is now most still, most secret, and most grave, / Who was in life a foolish prating knave" (3.4.214–16). To prate is to talk foolishly, as Hamlet is painfully conscious that that is what he is now doing, even if only to outmatch Laertes: "Nay, an thou'lt mouth, / I'll rant as well as thou" (5.1.283–84). He later apologizes to Horatio "That to Laertes I forgot myself, . . . But sure the bravery of his grief did put me / Into a tow'ring passion" (5.2.76, 79–80). "Bravery" (bravado) is the same word that Hamlet used to scoff at his own ranting soliloquy: "Why, what an ass am I! This is most brave" (2.2.589).

So Hamlet's advice to the players at the beginning of act 3, scene 2 is rooted in stylistic issues of the entire play. The basic point is that we expect Hamlet as actor to follow his own precepts. There is also an interesting self-referential point because the advice is also to Burbage who is playing Hamlet. It seems from what he says that Hamlet has been coaching the Player: "Speak the speech, I pray you, as I pronounced it to you, trippingly on the tongue" (3.2.1–2). Hamlet seems to be speaking of "a speech of some dozen or sixteen lines which I would set down and insert in't" (2.2.547–48) into *The Murder of Gonzago*. This is the most extensive discussion of acting in all of Shakespeare, and the repeated message is that the acting should be natural, that "you o'erstep not the modesty of nature" (3.2.19). Hamlet defines the purpose of playing as "to hold, as 'twere, the mirror up to nature; to show virtue her own feature, scorn her own image, and the very age and body of the time his form and pressure" (3.2.21–24). Also, there is a strong prohibition against ad-libbing, especially for the clowns (or fools): "And let those that play your clowns speak no more than is set down for them" (3.2.38–40). The advice to the players sets up standards for acting that are obviously contradicted by the prating Polonius, by the ranting Laertes and Hamlet himself, and by the absurdly precious Osric. So *Hamlet* contains within itself a set of criteria by which we can make stylistic judgments.

Hamlet shows himself extremely knowledgeable about what is happening in the theater of Shakespeare's own time. He seems to have a joking relation with the actors as he remembers items from the past: "Welcome, good friends. O, old friend, why, thy face is valanced [fringed with a beard] since I saw thee last. Com'st thou to beard me in Denmark?" (2.2.429–31). And to the boy actor who played female roles: "By'r Lady, your ladyship is nearer to heaven than when I saw you last by the altitude of a chopine [shoe with a thick sole, probably of cork]. Pray God your voice, like a piece of uncurrent gold, be not cracked within the ring" (2.2.432–35). Hamlet says all the right things to indicate that he is comfortable with the players.

He asks the principal actor (usually called the First Player) to give him a sample, "a taste of your quality. Come, a passionate speech" (2.2.438–39). He specifies exactly what he has in mind: "I heard thee speak me a speech once, but it was never acted, or if it was, not above once, for the play, I remember, pleased not the million; 'twas caviary to the general" (2.2.441–44). Hamlet speaks like an insider—how does he happen to know about a play that was never acted or acted only once? The speech is Aeneas's tale to Dido, which may refer back to Marlowe's Dido play. And Hamlet, although he wanted the Player to give him "a taste of your quality," now proceeds to speak thirteen lines of a speech about "the rugged Pyrrhus" (2.2.459), which is then continued by the First Player. Polonius, who holds himself to be a connoisseur of theater, praises Hamlet's histrionic abilities: "Fore God, my lord, well spoken, with good accent and good discretion" (2.2.473–74). Presumably, the audience is meant to agree with Polonius about Hamlet's skill as an actor. This interlude about Aeneas's tale to Dido leads directly to Hamlet's passionate and ranting soliloquy, "O, what a rogue and peasant slave am I!" (2.2.555ff).

Once *The Mousetrap* play has been performed, Hamlet is ecstatic about how successful the play has been in revealing the guilty conscience of the king. This is a high point for Hamlet in the play. In his high spirits, he imagines that he could turn professional as an actor. As he asks Horatio so extravagantly: "Would not this, sir, and a forest of feathers—if the rest of my fortunes turn Turk with me—with two Provincial roses on my razed shoes, get me a fellowship in a cry [company] of players?" (3.2.279–82). Horatio, to curb his ardor, says: "Half a share," but Hamlet is confident about his great success: "A whole one, I" (3.2.283–84).

To continue with the acting imagery, Hamlet prepares for his meeting with his mother in act 3, scene 4 in a soliloquy at the end of act 3, scene 2. The point of this soliloquy is that Hamlet is thinking of himself as an actor preparing a role. After the success of *The Mousetrap*, Hamlet is steeling himself to take revenge for his father's murder. At this moment, he still thinks that his mother is complicit. He speaks in a towering passion like the First Player's version of Pyrrhus in Aeneas's tale to Dido (2.2.461f): "Now could I drink hot blood / And do such bitter business as the day / Would quake to look on" (3.2.398–400). This is like the ranting style of Hamlet's soliloquy at the end of act 2. The essential part of Hamlet's resolve before he meets with his mother is to prevent himself from murdering her:

> O heart, lose not thy nature; let not ever
> The soul of Nero [who actually murdered his mother] enter this firm bosom.
> Let me be cruel, not unnatural;
> I will speak daggers to her, but use none. (3.2.401–4)

Hamlet is certainly cruel to his mother in the closet scene (3.4), and she thinks he is intent on murdering her. This is what leads to the death of Polonius, stabbed by Hamlet while he is behind the arras.

Finally, in this survey of Hamlet as actor, we mustn't forget his most extensive role in the play: that of playing mad. It begins after he has spoken with the Ghost of his father. He resolves "To put an antic disposition on" (1.5.172). "Antic" means grotesque, fantastic, as in *Romeo and Juliet*, when Tybalt describes the masked Romeo as coming to the ball "covered with an antic face" (1.5.58). Hamlet is determined to play the madman as a way of protecting himself, of having, as it were, poetic license. He convinces the otherwise astute Polonius that he suffering "the very ecstasy of love" (2.1.102) for Ophelia. In his interchange with Polonius in act 2, scene 2, Hamlet wittily pursues his mad role without much changing the old counselor's opinion that "Though this be madness, yet there is method in't" (2.1.206–7) and further: "How pregnant sometimes his replies are! A happiness that often madness hits on, which reason and sanity could not so prosperously be delivered of" (2.1.210–13). After Hamlet's scene with Ophelia, the king is not persuaded that Hamlet is mad: "Love? His affections do not that way tend, / Nor what he spake, though it lacked form a little, / Was not like madness" (3.1.163–65). The king is convinced that Hamlet's melancholy is dangerous, that he must suspect Claudius of the murder of his brother, and that he must be sent at once to England to be executed. His final, menacing line in this scene is: "Madness in great ones must not unwatched go" (3.1.190).

Hamlet continues to alternate between his normal style and his mad role for the rest of the play. During *The Murder of Gonzago*, he is particularly active in displaying his antic disposition. As he says when the king and queen and their court enter: "They are coming to the play: I must be idle" (3.2.90). "Idle" is often a word used specifically for the fool or clown, indicating silly or mad behavior. Hamlet uses his "idle" manner to insult Ophelia with grossly sexual and vulgar remarks. He asks: "Lady, shall I lie in your lap?", "I mean, my head upon your lap?," "Do you think I meant country matters?" (3.2.112, 115, 117). "Country" may be an imagined adjectival form of "cunt," as in Iago's explicitly sexual pun in *Othello*: "I know our country disposition well: / In Venice they do let heaven see the pranks / They dare not show their husbands" (3.3.201–3).

Hamlet assumes the role of commentator on the play. When Ophelia asks "What means this, my lord?" he replies "Marry, this is miching mallecho; it means mischief" (3.2.139–41). This is an odd and extravagant phrase, used only once in Shakespeare and much disputed about its exact meaning and origin. Hamlet continues to make remarks—personal remarks—throughout the play, as if he were its author. When the king asks naively "Have you heard the argument? Is there no offense in't?" (3.2.236–37), Hamlet answers with ironic jubilation: "No, no, they do but jest, poison in jest; no offense i' th' world" (3.2.238–39). It seems as if, in his idle fit, Hamlet is taking charge of the performance. He is impatient with the slowness of Lucianus: "Begin, murderer. Leave thy damnable faces and begin. Come, the croaking raven doth bellow for revenge" (3.2.256–58). Hamlet seems to be writing the line itself about the raven, which is not spoken by any of the actors.

We could go on with Hamlet's scene with Rosencrantz and Guildenstern, who take him to certain death in England. As Hamlet reports it to Horatio, it all seems histrionic: "Being thus benetted round with villains, / Or [ere] I could make a prologue to my brains, / They had begun the play" (5.2.29–31). The language is theatrical. The incident is also phrased in providential language:

> Rashly,
> (And praised be rashness for it) let us know,
> Our indiscretion sometime serves us well
> When our deep plots do pall, and that should learn us
> There's a divinity that shapes our ends,
> Rough-hew them how we will. (5.2.6–11)

So the idea of Hamlet's playing a role, or roles, in this play is also mixed in with the idea that he is directed by Providence. God the carpenter is shaping the ends that we can only rough-hew. I don't mean to imply that this is a God-directed play, but Hamlet's acting is pervasive throughout, although it cannot manage to outwit the king and Laertes's nefarious and many-headed plot against his life.

# Chapter Twenty

# Sex Nausea in
*Troilus and Cressida*

There is an attempt in *Troilus and Cressida* to make the Trojan War seem anti-heroic and anti-romantic. Shakespeare is intent on undermining the heroic tradition of Homer's *Iliad*. The heroic figures of the Trojan War are meant to seem slightly foolish, and the lovers, like Troilus, are so excessive in their ardor as to appear remote from the world. The genre of *Troilus and Cressida* is also puzzling. Because of the death of Hector, it seems more of a tragedy than anything else, in the mode of the history plays. But it also has a great deal of satire, especially by such a scurrilous character as Thersites. Some critics would like to think of it as a comical satire, like the plays Marston, Jonson, and others were writing.

Paris's abduction of Helen from her husband Menelaus is at the root of the Trojan War. In the middle of the play (3.1), we see Helen and Paris in a domestic scene, visited by Pandarus, the uncle of Cressida. We are struck by how comfortable everybody is. Pandarus greets Helen and Paris with overly elaborate courtesy, much in the manner of Polonius in *Hamlet*: "Fair be to you, my lord, and to all this fair company. Fair desires in all fair measure fairly guide them. Especially to you, fair queen, fair thoughts be your fair pillow" (3.1.44–47). This is courtly discourse in the parodic vein, which Helen continues: "Dear lord, you are full of fair words" (3.1.48). But Pandarus is not to be outdone: "You speak your fair pleasure, sweet queen" (3.1.49–50). This is all fairly ridiculous, but we are drawn into the homely scene by the fact that everyone is so much at ease—Paris even addresses Helen by her nickname, Nell. They insist that Pandarus sing a song about love.

The characters in this scene are all sophisticated, and their discourse is full of sexual double-entendres. Pandarus says: "My niece is horribly in love with a thing you have, sweet queen" (3.1.97–98). "Thing" is ambiguously sexual, but it probably refers to Paris as Helen's lover. In reply to Pandarus's insistence that Troilus and Cressida are "twain" (3.1.102), or at odds, Helen delivers a bawdy joke: "Falling in, after falling out, may make them three" (3.1.103–4). So we are amply prepared for Pandarus's love song. Helen says: "Let thy song be love. This love will undo us all. O Cupid, Cupid, Cupid!" (3.1.110–11), and Paris announces the title: "Love, love, nothing but love" (3.1.113).

Pandarus's song turns on the sexual pun on "die," meaning to have an orgasm, and cries connected with sexual climax:

> These lovers cry, O ho! They die!
> Yet that which seems the wound to kill
> Doth turn O ho! to Ha, ha, he!
> So dying love lives still.
> O ho! a while, but Ha, ha, ha!
> O ho! groans out for Ha, ha, ha!—Heigh ho! (3.1.119–24)

Pandarus's bawdy song fits well with the scene of Helen in Paris's household.

In answer to Paris's "hot deeds is love" (3.1.128), Pandarus elaborates on what strikes us as a central theme of the play: "Is this the generation of love—hot blood, hot thoughts, and hot deeds? Why, they are vipers. Is love a generation of vipers?" (3.1.129–31). The passage strongly echoes Matthew in the New Testament and is meant to ground the anti-romantic bias of the play. Pandarus's song may be "Love, love, nothing but love," but love is ultimately bitter and tormenting.

Let us go back to the beginning of the play, to Troilus's mooning desire to make love with Cressida. The passion is excessive, as if love were a fever. Cressida's uncle, Pandarus, the go-between, tries to bring Troilus to patience in his furious suit by imagery drawn from making a cake: "He that will have a cake out of the wheat must tarry the grinding" (1.1.14–16). The abundant food and animal imagery to express sexual themes runs counter to Troilus's elevated expressions, but these sometimes go astray, as if Troilus cannot restrain his stylistic copiousness, as in the following grotesque passage:

> I tell thee I am mad
> In Cressid's love; thou answer'st she is fair.
> Pour'st in the open ulcer of my heart
> Her eyes, her hair, her cheek, her gait, her voice. (1.1.53–56)

The open ulcer of Troilus's heart is hardly a romantic image, and the idea of Pandarus pouring in all of Cressida's admirable qualities is equally inappropriate, as is Troilus's concluding lines: "Thou lay'st in every gash that love hath given me / The knife that made it" (1.1.64–65).

In act 3, scene 2, where Troilus and Cressida consummate their love, Troilus, at the beginning of the scene, is still the hopelessly lovesick youth he is in the first scene of the play. His language and imagery, however, are still strangely inappropriate to their context. Why does he ask Pandarus, the go-between, to be his ferryman over the river Styx to Hades or hell? Why does he already have forebodings that his love affair will have an infernal side to it? His first speech to Pandarus is already dire:

> O, be thou my Charon,
> And give me swift transportation to those fields
> Where I may wallow in the lily beds
> Proposed for the deserver. (3.2.9–12)

Why "wallow," which is an oddly negative word for a true lover?

In his soliloquy after Pandarus leaves, Troilus expresses his fears of sexual consummation. Admittedly, "Th imaginary relish is so sweet / That it enchants my sense" (3.2.17–18), but orgasmic fulfillment scares Troilus:

> What will it be
> When that the wat'ry [watering] palates taste indeed
> Love's thrice-repurèd nectar? Death, I fear me,
> Sounding [swooning] destruction, or some joy too fine,
> Too subtle, potent, tuned too sharp in sweetness
> For the capacity of my ruder powers.
> I fear it much. (3.2.18–24)

Troilus's apprehensions are like those in Sonnet 129, "Th' expense of spirit in a waste of shame." The sonnet speaks frankly about lust, a word never used by Troilus, but the mood is the same: "A bliss in proof, and proved, a very woe, / Before, a joy proposed; behind, a dream." It is possible that this sonnet and *Troilus and Cressida* were written around the same time. Troilus continues to develop negative imagery for the act of love, which is almost certain to be disappointing: "This is the monstruosity in love, lady, that the will is infinite and the execution confined; that the desire is boundless and the act a slave to limit" (3.2.80–82). So we are prepared, in a way, for the bad outcome of this love affair.

Cressida in love is represented differently from Troilus. In her early soliloquy in act 1, scene 2, her mannered couplets express her calculation and cunning: "Yet hold I off. Women are angels, wooing; / Things won are done, joy's soul lies in the doing" (1.2.293–94). Her plan is to manipulate Troilus's ardor. I think we are surprised at how moralistic Cressida's couplets sound. This kind of practical thinking about amorous conduct certainly doesn't make Cressida seem like a woman in love. Her advice to herself is abundantly didactic: "That she beloved knows nought that knows not this: / Men prize the thing ungained more than it is" (1.2.295–96). She teaches a maxim out of love doctrine: "Achievement is command; ungained, beseech" (1.2.300). It is important that we have these bald assertions from Cressida early in the play.

In the scene leading up to the consummation of their affair, Cressida is similarly coy and flirtatious, although there is no doubt about the outcome of Pandarus's endeavors. He makes no effort to conceal the fact that he is a pimp, or pander. Cressida's bantering conversation with Troilus mocks male bravado:

> They say all lovers swear more performance than they are able, and yet reserve an ability that they never perform, vowing more than the perfection of ten and discharging less than the tenth part of one. They that have the voice of lions and the act of hares—are they not monsters? (3.2.86–91)

This kind of sophisticated discourse does not seem promising in wooing the already inflamed Troilus, who defends the male gender.

Cressida's confession of love for Troilus, a love that she claims was long in preparation, rings hollow because she sticks to the kind of feminine wiles that were already apparent in her soliloquy in act 1, scene 2. She was

> Hard to seem won; but I was won, my lord,
> With the first glance that ever—pardon me;
> If I confess much you will play the tyrant.
> I love you now, but, till now, not so much
> But I might master it. (3.2.116–20)

The elaboration of Cressida's reasoning seems unconvincing:

> In faith, I lie;
> My thoughts were like unbridled children grown
> Too headstrong for their mother. See, we fools!
> Why have I blabbed? Who shall be true to us
> When we are so unsecret to ourselves? (3.2.120–24)

We tend to be shocked by Cressida's explicit, self-regarding comments that seem to tease Troilus's unmitigated passion: "Perchance, my lord, I show more craft than love, / And fell so roundly to a large confession / To angle for your thoughts" (3.2.151–53). But Troilus makes no attempt to match his lover's reasoning, or even to understand it fully. If we think about Cressida's words in this scene, it all bodes badly for the future.

We should not be surprised that Cressida is so flirtatious when she comes to the Greek camp and meets the principal officers. She offers kisses all around. Ulysses banters with her: "Why, then, for Venus' sake, give me a kiss, / When Helen is a maid again, and his [Menelaus's]" (4.5.49–50). Ulysses is the only one who refuses to kiss Cressida. He elaborates on Nestor's observation that she is "A woman of quick sense" (4.5.54)—in other words of a lively sexuality: "There's language in her eye, her cheek, her lip; / Nay, her foot speaks. Her wanton spirits look out / At every joint and motive [movement] of her body" (4.5.55–57). "Her foot speaks" is an extreme metaphor for Cressida's wantonness, or her provocative sexuality. Ulysses's long speech gets even more specific about Cressida's whorishness:

> O, these encounterers, so glib of tongue,
> That give a coasting welcome ere it comes,
> And wide unclasp the tables of their thoughts
> To every ticklish reader, set them down
> For sluttish spoils of opportunity
> And daughters of the game. (4.5.58–63)

A daughter of the game is a prostitute, but Cressida is represented as particularly appealing to "ticklish," or prurient, customers. She is a glib encounterer, who knows how to stimulate sexual appetite. There is a clever pun in the cry "The Troyans' trumpet" to announce the entrance of "*all of Troy*" (4.5.63 s.d.) after Ulysses's speech. "Trumpet" and "strumpet" make an easy phonetic pun.

Act 5, scene 2, the seduction of Cressida by Diomedes, is one of the most memorable big scenes in Shakespeare because it has not only Cressida wooed by Diomedes but also Troilus accompanied by Ulysses as observers, as well as the debasing sexual commentary of Thersites. The scene seems to proceed, therefore, on three different levels. When Cressida enters and whispers with Diomedes, we have Troilus's bitter "Yea, so familiar!" (5.2.8), followed by Ulysses's grosser observation, "She will sing any man at first sight" (5.2.9), concluded by Thersites's blatantly sexual remark, "And any man may sing her, if he can take her cliff; she's noted" (5.2.10–11). "Cliff" is an obvious sexual pun on "cleft," or pudendum, and "noted" continues the musical pun: she is a woman of ill repute. This kind of triple interplay continues throughout the scene.

Troilus cannot deal with the obviously false romantic image he has conjured up for Cressida. When she exits after Diomedes, Troilus grapples with the new reality to a sympathetic Ulysses: "This she? No, this is Diomed's Cressida" (5.2.134). Troilus's long and heartfelt reasonings try to understand what has happened to him, as if the reality he assumed has disappeared:

> Cressid is mine, tied with the bonds of heaven.
> Instance, O instance, strong as heaven itself;
> The bonds of heaven are slipped, dissolved, and loosed,
> And with another knot, five-finger-tied,

The fractions of her faith, orts of her love,
The fragments, scraps, the bits, and greasy relics
Of her o'ereaten faith, are given to Diomed. (5.2.152–58)

Troilus's imagination follows that of Thersites in using disgusting images of food, especially the scraps left over after the meal is finished. This is a far cry from his earlier sense of Cressida's lyric perfection.

Thersites, the scurrilous commentator, like Apemantus in *Timon of Athens*, does a great deal to develop the anti-heroic, anti-romantic tone of *Troilus and Cressida*. In this climactic scene (5.2), he echoes and further debases Troilus's comments. For example, he invokes one of the seven deadly sins to establish what is happening between Cressida and Diomedes: "How the devil Luxury, with his fat rump and potato finger, tickles these together. Fry, lechery, fry!" (5.2.54–56). This is the same greasy food imagery that Troilus has been using—potatoes were thought to be an aphrodisiac. At the very end of the scene, Thersites concludes with a reflection on the Trojan War: "Lechery, lechery; still wars and lechery; nothing else holds fashion. A burning devil take them!" (5.2192–94). "Burning devil" refers to the venereal disease that follows from lechery.

Thersites's reference to venereal disease is taken up by Pandarus in what seems to be his epilogue at the end of the play. He addresses the panders and bawds in the audience:

Good traders in the flesh, set this in your painted cloths:
"As many as be here of Pandar's hall,
Your eyes, half out, weep out at Pandar's fall;
Or if you cannot weep, yet give some groans,
Though not for me, yet for your aching bones." (5.10.44–49)

The bone ache and the sweating tub are all connected with venereal disease and its treatment. Pandarus is addressing panders and members of the "hold-door trade" (5.10.50), or prostitutes. The "painted cloths," probably with erotic scenes, were used to ornament brothels.

## Chapter Twenty-One

# Parolles the Braggart in
# *All's Well That Ends Well*

Like Falstaff in the *Henry IV* plays, Parolles, the man of words, is a "miles gloriosus" (a military braggart), a fluent speaker but an errant coward. He is also identified in this play as wearing a flamboyant costume that is meant purely for show. Everyone in the play except for Bertram recognizes him as a liar and a rogue, which tells us something important about the credulousness and immaturity of Bertram. Near the beginning of the play, Helena apologizes for him because of her love for Bertram: "I love him [Parolles] for his [Bertram's] sake, / And yet I know him a notorious liar, / Think him a great way fool, solely a coward" (1.1.102–4). From the start, there is no ambiguity about Parolles; there is nothing to discover about him that we don't begin with. Helena says that he has "some stain of soldier" (1.1.117), and, in the curious dialogue about virginity that follows, Parolles speaks fluently in traditional military images.

All of his advice to Bertram is misguided, especially his counsel to leave the court—against the king's specific command—and go to the wars in Italy. Like Osric in *Hamlet*, he affects a courtly and elaborate style that much impresses Bertram (but no one else). Before Bertram leaves, Parolles addresses members of the court in his best grandiloquent style:

> Noble heroes, my sword and yours are kin. Good sparks and lustrous, a word, good metals. You shall find in the regiment of the Spinii one Captain Spurio, with his cicatrice, an emblem of war, here on his sinister cheek; it was this very sword entrenched it. Say to him I live, and observe his reports for me.
> (2.1.42–48)

Of course, Captain Spurio is spurious, a figment of Parolles's vivid imagination.

Parolles's style is high-flown, at times almost parodic, and he imitates what he takes to be the language of the court. He uses a number of Italian (or italianate) expressions that have little to do with the context. For example, after he has advised Bertram to go to the wars and leave his new wife, he asks: "Will this capriccio hold in thee?" (2.3.296). This is the only example of the word in Shakespeare. At the end of act 2, scene 5, Parolles encourages Bertram with a parting exclamation: "Bravely, coragio!" (2.5.93). Bertram may be impressed, but does he even understand what his mentor is saying? There is a similar extravagant (but meaningless) oath when Parolles first sees Helena in 2.3: "Mor du vinager! Is not this Helen?" (2.3.45). The "death of vinegar" is pseudo-French and ridiculous in itself as a resounding oath.

We may note one other Parollesism toward the end of this same scene:

> To th' wars, my boy, to th' wars!
> He wears his honor in a box unseen,
> That hugs his kicky-wicky here at home,
> Spending his manly marrow in her arms,
> Which should sustain the bound and high curvet
> Of Mars's fiery steed. (2.3.281–86)

"Kicky-wicky" may be a bawdy word derived from the French "quelque-chose."

Everyone in the play (except for Bertram) is unimpressed by Parolles, but the old Lord Lafew is particularly insightful. He admits that Parolles "didst make tolerable vent of thy travel" (2.3.204–5), "vent" meaning copious talk, yet he is an obvious fake, as indicated by his absurd costume: "Yet the scarves and the bannerets about thee did manifoldly dissuade me from believing thee a vessel of too great burden" (2.3.205–7). The plethora of scarves Parolles wears is a parody of military dress. Lafew also calls him a "window of lattice" (2.3.215), a reference to a common tavern window. Parolles is grievously insulted, but he has no way of replying to Lafew. He pockets it all up with characteristic patience: "there is no fettering of authority" (2.3.239). Lafew is unsuccessful in convincing Bertram about Parolles, but he makes a heroic effort to unmask him: "Fare you well, my lord, and believe this of me, there can be no kernel in this nut; the soul of this man is his clothes" (2.5.42–44). Bertram seems impenetrable to the advice of his elders.

Parolles is convincingly exposed as a "counterfeit" (4.3.34) in the scene of the drum, when he is captured by his own soldiers in disguise. Bertram is present to witness his mentor revealing the secrets of his camp. As the First Lord says ironically: "Y' are deceived, my lord; this is Monsieur Parolles, the gallant militarist—that was his own phrase—that had the whole theoric

of war in the knot of his scarf, and the practice in the chape of his dagger"
(4.3.143–47).

Bertram is finally convinced that Parolles is a rogue when he is directly
insulted. Parolles calls him "a foolish idle boy, but for all that very ruttish
[lustful]" (4.3.220–21), and "a dangerous and lascivious boy, who is a whale
to virginity, and devours up all the fry it finds" (4.3.225–26). Parolles proves
to be a calumniator like Lucio in *Measure for Measure*, and Bertram cannot
contain his indignation: "Damnable both-sides rogue!" (4.3.227).

The remarkable thing about Parolles is that his unmasking seems to have
little effect on him. He is notably resilient when he abandons his military
role. His soliloquy at the end of this scene is surprisingly insightful:

> If my heart were great
> 'Twould burst at this. Captain I'll be no more,
> But I will eat and drink and sleep as soft
> As captain shall. Simply the thing I am
> Shall make me live. (4.3.344–38)

Parolles recognizes that "the thing I am" is an impostor. He is aware that he
has been playing a role, and he is doubly aware that there are many other
roles he can play that "Shall make me live." He goes on to comment on his
failed braggart part:

> Who knows himself a braggart,
> Let him fear this; for it will come to pass
> That every braggart shall be found an ass.
> Rust, sword; cool, blushes; and Parolles live
> Safest in shame! Being fooled, by fool'ry thrive!
> There's place and means for every man alive. (4.3.338–43)

The important thing for Parolles is to stay alive by whatever means it takes.
He is not at all abashed or apologetic for his deceit. Those who were deceived were more fools than he was. Parolles is almost a sympathetic character at this point.

At the end of the play, as in *Measure for Measure*, all is forgiven by the
folktale formula of "All's Well That Ends Well." Even Lafew is kind to
Parolles, who seems to be thankful to him for being the first to find him out.
Parolles, however, insists on some favors from Lafew: "It lies in you, my
lord, to bring me in some grace, for you did bring me out" (5.2.46–47).
Lafew is puzzled about what role he is being asked to play: "Out upon thee,
knave! Dost thou put upon me at once both the office of God and the devil?
One brings thee in grace and the other brings thee out" (5.2.48–50). But

Lafew does not abandon Parolles. He promises him "though you are a fool and a knave you shall eat" (5.2.56–57). So we end the play with Parolles seeming like a sympathetic character. His faults were clearly venal and came from a love of show rather than from any sense of evil-doing.

# Chapter Twenty-Two

# Iago's and Othello's "Ha's"

In the first scene of *Othello*, Iago's style is established. He speaks like a soldier, directly and without circumlocution or flourishes. He is fluent in the way he presents himself, often using informal, colloquial expressions. At times, he sprinkles his discourse with mild oaths and interjections, like "'Sblood" (by God's blood) (1.1.4), "Forsooth" (1.1.16), and "Zounds" (by God's wounds) (1.1.83, 105). In stirring up the anger of Brabantio, Desdemona's father, Iago does not hesitate to resort to vulgar, bestial sexual images like "an old black ram / Is tupping your white ewe" (1.1.85–86), and "you'll have your daughter covered with a Barbary horse" (1.1.107–8)— allusions to Othello's blackness—and "your daughter and the Moor are making the beast with two backs" (1.1.112–14). It is not surprising that Brabantio, the old father awakened from his sleep by rude shouting in the street, should ask Iago "What profane wretch art thou?" (1.1.111). Like the cunning villain that he is, Iago specializes in sowing discord and chaos. His characteristic style is evident in the first scene in his conversation with his gull Roderigo (like Sir Toby and his dupe Sir Andrew in *Twelfth Night*). There is the beginning in this scene of the ironic insistence on the word "honest" (and related forms), of which there is an avalanche of repetitions in *Othello*, as there also is in *Julius Caesar*.

Iago clearly wants to distinguish his "honest" style of speech from that of Othello, who evades the suitors for Iago's promotion "with a bombast circumstance, / Horribly stuffed with epithets of war" (1.1.12–13). Bombast is cotton used to stuff or line clothing, in other words, used to pad it out. Iago is contemptuous of Othello's high-flown style—formal, rhetorical, and with long, carefully composed periods. He doesn't speak like a soldier, even though Othello claims "Rude am I in my speech, / And little blessed with the soft phrase of peace" (1.3.81–82). Iago doesn't believe this at all. Of course,

Cassio, whom Othello has chosen as his lieutenant, is "Mere prattle without practice" (1.1.23)—a man of words, a theoretician, without any practical experience on the battlefield. Therefore, Iago resolves upon his duplicitous course: "I follow him to serve my turn upon him" (1.1.39). He firmly establishes his relation to Othello from the beginning of the play: "But I will wear my heart upon my sleeve / For daws to peck at; I am not what I am" (1.1.61–62). In other words, Iago will pretend to be something other than what he is. He will present to the world a face of candor and honesty both in words and in deeds.

Othello's first speech clearly distinguishes his style from Iago's:

> I fetch my life and being
> From men of royal siege; and my demerits
> May speak unbonneted to as proud a fortune
> As this that I have reached. For know, Iago,
> But that I love the gentle Desdemona,
> I would not my unhousèd free condition
> Put into circumspection and confine
> For the seas' worth. (1.2.20–27)

Othello speaks formally and rhetorically, as if conscious of addressing a group of people. He uses a polysyllabic and latinate diction, very different from Iago's conversational style. This is abundantly clear in his address to Brabantio and his men, who come to arrest him: "Keep up your bright swords, for the dew will rust them. / Good signior, you shall more command with years / Than with your weapons" (1.2.58–60). In a dire situation, Othello speaks with a calm and lyric self-control. He doesn't succeed in pacifying Brabantio, but Brabantio doesn't dare to arrest him with the officers he has brought for that purpose.

Act 1, scene 3 shows Othello at his best. His account of his wooing of Desdemona is elaborately detailed and a grand speech, as witnessed by the duke's remark: "I think this tale would win my daughter too" (1.3.170). Brabantio is utterly confounded by Othello and by his own daughter. We see Iago in this scene, especially in his conversations with Roderigo, resorting to characteristic animal imagery. He scoffs at Roderigo's idle talk of killing himself: "Ere I would say I would drown myself for the love of a guinea hen, I would change my humanity with a baboon" (1.3.309–11). To Iago, all love is lust, and, like all of Shakespeare's villains, he puts an overwhelming emphasis on will: "Our bodies are our gardens, to the which our wills are gardeners" (1.3.315–16). Before the soliloquy that ends the scene, "sport" is another key word of Iago's. He tells Roderigo: "If thou canst cuckold him, thou dost thyself a pleasure, me a sport" (1.3.362–63). In the soliloquy itself, Iago apologizes to the audience for his attention to Roderigo: "For I mine own gained knowledge should profane / If I would time expend with such snipe / But for my sport and profit" (1.3.373–75). "Snipe" is a foolish bird, a woodcock, easily caught, and "snipe" is synonymous with fool or dupe. Iago's "sport" identifies him with the joking Vice figure of the medieval morality plays.

It is not until act 3, scene 3—practically in the middle of the play—that Othello fully engages with Iago. As soon as Cassio exits from his meeting with Desdemona, who has promised to plead his case for reinstatement as Othello's lieutenant, Iago skillfully plants a doubt in Othello's mind: "Ha! I like not that" (3.3.34). "Ha" is an emotionally loaded interjection expressing surprise or wonder, usually with negative connotations. "Ha" has no specific meaning except what is implied in the context. Iago's exclamation indicates that he is disturbed by Cassio's parting from Desdemona. He expresses a strong reaction, but, characteristically, he never says directly what it is he doesn't like about it. He forces Othello into a series of questions and disturbing efforts to penetrate his implications. Again, this is an uncharacteristic stylistic mode for Othello. His immediate reaction to Iago is "What dost thou say?" (3.3.35), which seems to mean not that he hasn't heard what Iago has just said but that he cannot fathom what Iago could mean by his provocative "Ha!" He is immediately thrown into the disturbing predicament of trying to find out what Iago really means but refuses to specify. This, of course, lies at the heart of this scene, in which Iago seduces his unsuspecting captain for his own nefarious purposes.

Othello's tragic vulnerability is defined by Iago in his soliloquy at the end of act 1, scene 3:

> The Moor is of a free and open nature
> That thinks men honest that but seem to be so;
> And will as tenderly be led by th' nose
> As asses are. (1.3.388–91)

Iago gloats over what is to be his successful—and easy—seduction of Othello in act 3, scene 3. He is confident that it won't be difficult.

After Iago's exclamation "Ha! I like not that," his speeches—or perhaps only his broken exclamations and insinuations—continue to provoke the "free and open" Othello. When he asks Iago to explain what he doesn't like about Cassio and Desdemona, Iago puts him off with a nonanswer: "Nothing, my lord; or if—I know not what" (3.3.36). Othello is at a loss to understand what Iago is implying, but he is sure that it is something bad. When he asks: "Was not that Cassio parted from my wife?" (3.3.37), Iago emphasizes his own doubts: "Cassio, my lord? No, sure, I cannot think it / That he would steal away so guilty-like, / Seeing your coming" (3.3.38–40). The question we want to ask is whether the Cassio we see on stage really "steal[s] away so guilty-like" when he sees Othello coming. It is the same issue that arises with the jealous Leontes in *The Winter's Tale*. Do we actually see Leontes's wife, Hermione, and his friend Polixenes "Kissing with inside lip" (1.2.286) and "Horsing foot on foot" (288)? I think not, but at least Leontes's fantasy is fed by his mad jealousy, whereas Iago's hints and insinuations are part of a crafty purpose to win over Othello.

When Desdemona exits, we already see Othello in deep perturbation from Iago's words: "Excellent wretch! Perdition catch my soul / But I do love thee! And when I love thee not, / Chaos is come again" (3.3.90–92). "Chaos" is used only six times in Shakespeare, always with a direly negative meaning. In Venus's complaint in *Venus and Adonis*, when Adonis is dead "with him is beauty slain, / And, beauty dead, black chaos comes again" (1019–20). In Ulysses's speech on degree in *Troilus and Cressida*, chaos follows "when degree is suffocate" (1.3.125). So Othello sees both perdition and chaos coming as a result of Iago's speeches. Notice how quickly he is persuaded by Iago and how profound his tragic vulnerability is.

The speech about chaos is followed by eight puzzled questions from Othello, who is now deeply troubled. He obviously cannot believe what Iago is implying, but he also cannot fathom what Iago is really saying. When Iago asks "Did Michael Cassio, when you wooed my lady, / Know of your love?" (3.3.94–95), Othello's only reply is the question "Why dost thou ask?" (3.3.96), as if he cannot make out what Iago is driving at. This is followed by "Why of thy thought, Iago?" (3.3.98), and "Indeed?" "Ay, indeed! Discern'st thou aught in that?, / Is he not honest?" (3.3.101–3). These lines have no relation to the language that Othello speaks earlier in the play—he is already being drawn into Iago's style.

The interchange between Iago and Othello that follows presents an almost meaningless verbal display in which the language conceals what the characters are thinking and feeling:

*Othello*. What dost thou think?

*Iago*. Think, my lord?

*Othello*. Think, my lord?

By heaven, thou echoest me,

As if there were some monster in thy thought

Too hideous to be shown. Thou dost mean something.

I heard thee say even now, thou lik'st not that,

When Cassio left my wife. What didst not like? (3.3.105–10)

Iago has no intention of showing Othello his "thought"; he says only—perfunctorily—"My lord, you know I love you" (3.3.117).

I think he enjoys tormenting Othello when he explains: "It were not for your quiet nor your good, / Nor for my manhood, honesty, and wisdom, / To let you know my thoughts" (3.3.152–54). But Othello is insistent: "By heaven, I'll know thy thoughts!" (3.3.162). It's no use pursuing the matter, and Iago is curtly dismissive: "You cannot, if my heart were in your hand; / Nor shall not whilst 'tis in my custody" (3.3.162–63). It is at this climactic point that Othello bursts out with sheer frustration: "Ha!" (3.3.164). "Ha" is a key word of Iago, who began this interchange with an observation about Cassios's leaving Desdemona: "Ha! I like not that."

So Othello has now clearly been caught up in Iago's style of discourse. His insistence on "proofs" is another sign that he has entered the Iago world of materiality, abandoning his own sense of high-mindedness and a feeling for spiritual love: "I'll see before I doubt; when I doubt, prove; / And on the proof there is no more but this: / Away at once with love or jealousy" (3.3.190–92). Othello's demand for "ocular proof" (3.3.357) plays right into Iago's hands, so that he really doesn't need Desdemona's handkerchief that Emilia has just found. Othello's imperious and threatening exclamation is just what Iago desires to work his mischief: "Make me to see't; or at the least so prove it / That the probation bear no hinge nor loop / To hang a doubt on—or woe upon thy life!" (3.3.361–63). Iago can easily answer Othello's angry "I'll have some proof" (3.3.383) with: "Would you, the supervisor, grossly gape on? / Behold her topped?" (392–93). The handkerchief then fits in perfectly with Othello's demand for proofs. Othello's puzzled exclamation a little earlier in the scene—"Ha! ha! False to me?" (3.3.330)—repeats the Iago word "ha" (3.3.35, 165) and strengthens his commitment to Iago and to Iago's plan to murder Desdemona. At the end of the scene, in a quasi-religious ceremony, Othello appoints Iago his lieutenant, and Iago replies ominously: "I am your own forever" (3.3.476).

We need to add only one other scene to strengthen our sense of how Othello takes over Iago's style. Act 4, scene 1 begins with a series of questions from the now very passive Othello. It replays act 3, scene 3 after Iago says "Ha! I like not that" (3.3.35). Othello casts himself in the role of an ignorant student questioning his master. The discourse just before Othello's epileptic fit is random and unpurposive:

*Othello.* What hath he [Cassio] said?

*Iago.* Why, that he did—I know not what he did.

*Othello.* What? what?

*Iago.* Lie—

*Othello.* With her?

*Iago.* With her, on her; what you will. (4.1.31–35)

It is at this point that Othello begins to speak disconnectedly, like a mad person who has abandoned syntax and sentence structure. Othello's "falling sickness" is like that of Julius Caesar in *Julius Caesar*. Othello echoes Iago's words: "Lie with her? Lie on her?—We say lie on her when they belie her.— Lie with her! Zounds, that's fulsome.—Handkerchief—confessions—hand-kerchief!" (4.1.36–39). When Cassio enters, Iago speaks professionally, as if he were Othello's doctor: "My lord is fall'n into an epilepsy. / This is his second fit; he had one yesterday" (4.1.51–52). And Iago advises Cassio about the remedy: "The lethargy must have his quiet course. / If not, he foams at mouth, and by and by / Breaks out to savage madness" (4.1.54–56).

Othello is transformed by the devious and poisonous Iago. He is not the person he was—not just in his language, but in his inner being.

## Chapter Twenty-Three

# Lucio the Calumniator in
# *Measure for Measure*

Lucio is described in the cast of characters as a "fantastic," which relates to his role in the play. He has no specific function in the court of Duke Vincentio other than as a hanger-on and commentator. "Fantastic" is derived from "fantasy," meaning that Lucio is a creature of Fancy, and therefore extravagant, capricious, and bizarre. It is difficult to define his practical function in the play. He is like the lunatic, the lover, and the poet described by Duke Theseus in *A Midsummer Night's Dream* as "of imagination all compact" (5.1.8), persons of "seething brains" and "shaping fantasies, that apprehend / More than cool reason ever comprehends" (5.1.4, 5–6). "Fantastical" is, in fact, a word that Lucio likes. He uses it twice to describe the absent duke: "It was a mad fantastical trick of him to steal from the state, and usurp the beggary he was never born to" (3.2.93–94). This is almost exactly what Apemantus, another calumniator, says of Timon of Athens: "Thou'dst courtier be again / Wert thou not beggar" (4.3.242–43). Lucio also calls Vincentio "the old fantastical duke of dark corners" (4.3.158–59).

Shakespeare's calumniators—Apemantus in *Timon of Athens*, Thersites in *Troilus and Cressida*, and Lucio in *Measure for Measure*—are mostly unpleasant truth-speakers. But what about Lucio? There is no way to confirm what he says about the duke in the play, although he is right on the mark about the icy Angelo. Is the duke a whoremonger, or at least someone who "had some feeling of the sport; he knew the service, and that instructed him to mercy" (3.2.120–21)? That is one of the interpretive puzzles of the play, but at least it complicates the duke's role and prevents us from seeing him as a god-given savior whose clever bed-trick clears up all difficulties in the action.

Lucio refuses to provide bail for Pompey, who is being sent to prison. It is remarkable how lighthearted he is in his rejection of his seeming friend: "No, indeed, will I not, Pompey, it is not the wear. I will pray Pompey, to increase your bondage. If you take it not patiently, why, your mettle is the more. Adieu, trusty Pompey. 'Bless you, friar'" (3.2.74–77). "Wear" is a clothing image, meaning "it is not in the present fashion," as in Jaques's admiring image for the clown Touchstone in *As You Like It*: "Motley's the only wear" (2.7.34). At the end of the play, Lucio is similarly noncommittal and unmotivated about his gross slanders of the duke, who asks with real feeling: "Wherein have I so deserved of you, / That you extol me thus?" (5.1.504–5). Lucio doesn't have plausible explanation but says only: "'Faith, my lord, I spoke it but according to the trick" (5.1.506–7). This is an odd use of the word "trick," meaning "custom, habit, or fashion." Lucio doesn't seem to want to justify himself, although what he does to soften the duke's compassion and restrain the wild excesses of Angelo promotes the best interests of the audience and the play.

Is Lucio just acting for his own amusement, like Puck in *A Midsummer Night's Dream* or the Vice-derived villains of Shakespearean tragedy, like Aaron in *Titus Andronicus*? But Lucio does act purposively on behalf of the play when, for example, he encourages Isabella in her pleas to Angelo for her brother's life. Claudio is convinced that his sister will be successful:

> for in her youth
> There is a prone and speechless dialect
> Such as move men; beside, she hath prosperous art
> When she will play with reason and discourse,
> And well she can persuade. (1.2.185–89)

There is already something suggestively erotic in Claudio's speech. Lucio undertakes to persuade Isabella to convince Angelo to spare her brother. His opening line is startling in its irreverence: "Hail virgin—if you be" (1.4.16).

In act 2, scene 2, Lucio is active in encouraging Isabella to be more passionate in her discourse with Angelo. One may well ask whether Lucio is the effective cause for Angelo's falling in love with Isabella. He repeats, "You are too cold" (2.2.45, 56), and says "Ay, touch him; there's the vein" (2.2.71). He eggs her on when he thinks she is getting warmer: "That's well said" (2.2.110), and "O, to him, to him, wench! He will relent; / He's coming; I perceive't" (2.2.125–26). One wonders what Isabella would do without Lucio cheering her on.

Lucio is obviously a truth-speaker in his account of the cold and hardhearted Angelo:

> Some report a sea maid spawned him; some, that he was begot between two stockfishes [dried cod]. But it is certain that when he makes water his urine is

congealed ice; that I know to be true. And he is a motion generative [masculine puppet]; that's infallible. (3.2.109–13)

The absent duke is quite different: "Ere he would have hanged a man for the getting a hundred bastards, he would have paid for the nursing a thousand. He had some feeling of the sport; he knew the service, and that instructed him to mercy" (3.2.118–21). The duke protests vigorously: "I never heard the absent duke much detected for women; he was not inclined that way" (3.2.124–25). This doesn't, of course, mean that the duke is a homosexual. Lucio claims to be an intimate friend of the duke, but he slanders him gratuitously nevertheless: "A very superficial, ignorant, unweighing fellow" (2.2.142). Lucio seems to have no particular direction in his comments, since he both praises and insults the duke almost at the same time.

When Lucio exits, the Duke expresses his bewilderment in some sententious observations:

No might nor greatness in mortality
Can censure 'scape; back-wounding calumny
The whitest virtue strikes. What king so strong
Can tie the gall up in the slanderous tongue? (2.2.185–88)

The duke obviously thinks well of himself, but he has no comprehension of Lucio, who is garrulous in his mixed praise and scorn. There is no getting rid of him. As he exclaims to the Friar: "I am a kind of burr; I shall stick" (4.3.180).

At the climax of the play in act 5, scene 1, Lucio seems unstoppable in his efforts to dominate the discourse. His calumny flows freely against the duke disguised as a friar: "Why, you bald-pated, lying rascal, you must be hooded, must you? Show your knave's visage, with a pox to you. Show your sheep-biting face, and be hanged an hour. Will't not off?" (5.1.354–58). It is at this point that Lucio pulls off the friar's hood and discovers the Duke.

What follows then for Lucio seems anticlimactic. The duke is particularly enraged and says he cannot pardon him, but, according to the formulas of mercy entailed by measure-for-measure, Lucio escapes with only having to marry Kate Keepdown, the whore he has got with child. He protests energetically: "Marrying a punk, my lord, is pressing to death, whipping, and hanging" (5.1.524–25), but the duke is adamant: "Slandering a prince deserves it" (5.1.526).

In the Haroun al-Rashid story that underlies *Measure for Measure*, there is always a near certainty that the story of the disguised ruler who surveys his kingdom will end badly. This is similar to tales of the husband who disguises himself in order to see whether his wife is faithful, on the model of patient Griselda. *Measure for Measure* doesn't end badly, but there is a certain absurdity in the testing of Angelo, since the duke already knows that Angelo has behaved badly in refusing to marry Mariana. The play is much more about the testing of the duke. In this enterprise, Lucio has a valuable role to play. Although he is a calumniator, Lucio hints at inadequacies in the duke's humanity. He shouldn't pretend to be cold like Angelo to test the integrity of his kingdom. Besides, he should have had enough sense not to appoint Angelo as a moral arbiter. Lucio is there for us to ask essential questions about the duke's role.

# Chapter Twenty-Four

# Madness in *King Lear*

Madness in Shakespeare provides a useful stylistic device for changing a character, providing him or her with a new inwardness and a much wider range of emotions. In *Titus Andronicus*, for example, Titus is highly distracted by the misfortunes he has suffered, but not quite mad. His perturbations endow him with new insight into the malign reality that surrounds him. He feels his sorrow deeply, and he serves as a model—in language also—for *King Lear*, written many years later. Ophelia, too, is transformed by madness into someone different from the obedient daughter of Polonius. She suddenly reveals herself as a more expressive, lyrical, erotic young woman. Her character is, as it were, opened up. The same is also true of Lady Macbeth, who, in her madness, exhibits an acute and painful awareness of her complicity in murder. At the end of *Macbeth*, she can no longer say, as she did after the murder of Duncan, "A little water clears us of this deed: / How easy is it then!" (2.2.66–67).

Similarly, in *King Lear*, the king in his madness comes to understand things about "Poor naked wretches" (3.4.28) that he ignored before:

> O, I have ta'en
> Too little care of this. Take physic, pomp,
> Expose thyself to feel what wretches feel,
> That thou mayst shake the superflux to them
> And show the heavens more just. (3.4.32–36)

Lear's madness—or incipient madness here—serves to expand and deepen his role from the petulant father's love contest in the first scene.

Lear's madness doesn't come upon him all at once. It proceeds by a series of recognizable steps. The first mention of the king's potential madness is in Kent's courageous rebuke of his rejection of Cordelia: "be Kent unmannerly

119

/ When Lear is mad. What wouldst thou do, old man?" (1.1.146–47). The seeds of Lear's eventual madness are already evident to Kent. The king is subject to "flattery," he has fallen to "folly," he is guilty of "hideous rashness" (1.1.149, 150, 152). Kent sees a fatal outcome from Lear's casting off the daughter he loves the most. At the end of this same scene, Goneril and Regan are convinced that their aging father is growing senile. Goneril says: "He always loved our sister most, and with what poor judgement he hath now cast her off appears too grossly" (1.1.292–93), and Regan supports her sister: "'Tis the infirmity of his age, yet he hath ever but slenderly known himself" (1.1.294–95). These comments in act 1 prepare us for Lear's eventual madness.

In act 1, scene 4, the Fool berates Lear on his folly, which has precipitated him into second childhood:

> thou mad'st thy daughters thy mothers; for when thou gav'st them the rod and
> putt's down thine own breeches,
> Then they for sudden joy did weep
> And I for sorrow sung,
> That such a king should play bo-peep,
> And go the fools among. (1.4.163–69)

The Fool persists in his satirical attack on Lear's misguided decision to give Goneril and Regan all and Cordelia nothing: "Thou hadst little wit in thy bald crown when thou gav'st thy golden one away" (1.4.155–56). The Fool pursues this theme relentlessly in his dialogue with the king. It is not until the next scene that the Fool prods Lear into an explicit recognition of his folly: "O let me not be mad, not mad, sweet heaven! I would not be mad. Keep me in temper, I would not be mad" (1.5.43–45). Lear's incipient madness is already evident from the beginning of the play.

By act 2, scene 2, Lear's passionate grief has intensified. After he discovers Kent in the stocks, put there by the cruel Cornwall, he can hardly control his outburst: "O, how this mother swells up toward my heart! / *Hysterica passio*, down, thou climbing sorrow, / Thy element's below" (2.2.246–48). Hysteria, familiarly called "the mother," was considered a disease of women that arose from the womb and caused a sense of suffocation in the throat. Lear, once assured of his own judgment, now feels that grief has overwhelmed him and he is choking. The mother is a "climbing sorrow." That is why Lear says to the Fool: "O me, my heart! My rising heart! But down!" (2.2.310). Lear is invoking the mother, rising from the womb and suffocating him, to descend to its rightful place below.

There are further mentions in this scene of Lear's oncoming madness, as he exclaims to Goneril: "Now I prithee, daughter, do not make me mad: / I will not trouble thee, my child. Farewell: / We'll no more meet, no more see one another" (2.2.407–9). When Regan also rejects him and he is cast out onto the barren heath, the king forswears tears, which are a woman's prerogative, and vows to avenge his wrongs:

No, I'll not weep. *Storm and tempest.*
I have full cause of weeping, but this heart
Shall break into a hundred thousand flaws
Or e'er I'll weep. O fool, I shall go mad. (2.2.472–75)

This leads to Lear's direct perception on the heath that his "wits begin to turn" (3.2.67). This is close to what Kent says in a later scene: "His wits begin t'unsettle" (3.4.158).

The point is that Lear doesn't go mad all at once. Even on the heath, he is in the process of going mad. As Gloucester puts it: "the King grows mad" (3.4.161). Lear himself is aware that his mind is grievously affected by his sorrows: "this tempest in my mind / Doth from my senses take all feeling else, / Save what beats there, filial ingratitude" (3.4.12–14). It is significant that Lear himself understands that his preoccupation with the cruelty of Goneril and Regan will render him lunatic:

O, Regan, Goneril,
Your old, kind father, whose frank heart gave you all—
O, that way madness lies, let me shun that;
No more of that. (3.4.19–22)

But, of course, Lear has no way of shunning the bitter reality in which he is enveloped.

The king is not fully mad until act 4, scene 6, and it is interesting that this is the only scene in the play that shows him so. There is a conclusive stage direction from the Quarto: "*Enter* LEAR *mad*" (4.6.80). When he is approached by a Gentleman and two attendants from Cordelia, he says meaningfully: "Let me have surgeons, / I am cut to the brains" (4.6.188–89). Lear's discourse in this scene is scattered and wandering, like that of Lady Macbeth. He speaks distractedly in prose, jumping from subject to subject in matters that preoccupy him:

No, they cannot touch me for coining. I am the King himself . . . Nature's above art in that respect. There's your press-money. That fellow handles his bow like a crow-keeper: draw me a clothier's yard. Look, look, a mouse: peace, peace, this piece of toasted cheese will do't. (4.6.83–89)

When he meets Gloucester, his speech becomes more focussed: "Ha! Goneril with a white beard? They flattered me like a dog and told me I had the white hairs in my beard ere the black ones were there" (4.6.96–98). When Gloucester asks: "Is't not the King?" Lear replies "Ay, every inch a king"

(4.6.106). He is preoccupied with justice and hypocrisy in some of the most eloquent speeches in the play: "Let copulation thrive" (4.6.112) and "Robes and furred gowns hide all" (4.6.161).

He seems to recognize the blind Gloucester: "I remember thine eyes well enough. Dost thou squiny [squint] at me? / No, do thy worst, blind Cupid, I'll not love. / Read thou this challenge, mark but the penning of it" (4.6.132–35). And later: "If thou wilt weep my fortunes, take my eyes. / I know thee well enough, thy name is Gloucester" (4.6.172–73). Is Lear already recovering his sanity (as he will do in later scenes)? As Edgar says, aside: "O matter and impertinancy mixed, / Reason in madness" (4.6.170–71). Stylistically, his madness allows Lear to speak with a new intensity and inwardness about the state of the world.

Once he is rescued by Cordelia and her attendants at the end of act 4, scene 6, the next scene is devoted to his restoration. Cordelia is optimistic as she prays to the gods to "Cure this great breach in his abused nature; / Th'untuned and jarring senses, O, wind up / Of this child-changed father" (4.7.15–17). Cordelia's musical images are acted out in the music that is played to cure Lear's "jarring senses." We think of the importance of music in the statue scene in *The Winter's Tale* (5.3); Paulina actually says to the statue: "Music, awake her: strike" (5.3.98).

We saw the mad Lear in the previous scene enter *"crowned with wild flowers"* (4.6.80 s.d.). Now Cordelia's attendants have "put fresh garments on him" (4.7.22). When he awakes, he speaks hesitantly as if he is not in this world:

> You do me wrong to take me out o'the grave.
> Thou art a soul in bliss, but I am bound
> Upon a wheel of fire that mine own tears
> Do scald like molten lead. (4.7.45–48)

His restoration is gradual. He no longer speaks in the intense, emotional discourse of the previous scene. His diction is simple, and his tone declarative:

> Pray do not mock me.
> I am a very foolish, fond old man,
> Fourscore and upward, not an hour more nor less;
> And to deal plainly,
> I fear I am not in my perfect mind. (4.7.59–63)

Notice that in this context he doesn't speak in the persona of the king. In the same direct style, he comes to recognize his lost child: "Do not laugh at me, / For, as I am a man, I think this lady / To be my child Cordelia" (4.7.68–70). Cordelia matches his speech when she acknowledges her presence: "And so I am, I am" (4.7.70). Cordelia's Gentleman speaks as an insightful psychologist:

> the great rage
> You see is killed in him, and yet it is danger
> To make him even o'er the time he has lost.
> Desire him to go in. Trouble him no more
> Till further settling. (4.7.78–82)

So, Lear, although he is now sane, is still in a delicate condition. It is interesting that in Shakespeare only Lear and the Jailer's Daughter in *The Two Noble Kinsmen* are cured of their madness.

Edgar in *King Lear* assumes the role of Poor Tom, a mad Bedlam beggar, to escape from his brother Edmund's plot against his life:

> While I may scape
> I will preserve myself, and am bethought
> To take the basest and most poorest shape
> That ever penury in contempt of man
> Brought near to beast. (2.2.176–80)

Bedlam beggars "Enforce their charity" "Sometime with lunatic bans [curses], sometime with prayers" (2.2.191, 190). Edgar, the feigned madman, is set against King Lear, who is going mad; it makes for a significant contrast, especially in act 3, scene 4 on the heath.

Edgar is convincing in his role as the mad beggar tormented by fiends. Lear conceives him as a fellow sufferer: "Didst thou give all to thy two daughters? And art thou come to this?" (3.4.48–49). He sees in Poor Tom an image of his own debased condition:

> Is man no more than this? Consider him well. Thou ow'st the worm no silk, the beast no hide, the sheep no wool, the cat no perfume. Ha? Here's three on's are sophisticated; thou art the thing itself. Unaccomodated man is no more but such a poor, bare, forked animal as thou art. (3.4.101–6)

It is at this point that Lear begins to tear off his clothes: "Off, off, you lendings: come, unbutton here" (3.4.106–7). He wants to follow the example of Poor Tom as "unaccomodated man." Later, Lear insists on speaking with him as a natural "philosopher," a "learned Theban" (3.4.150, 153). This is probably a reference to the Cynic philosopher Diogenes. So Edgar, playing to the hilt the role of Poor Tom, provides Lear with a mirror image of his own perturbations.

To Gloucester, too, Edgar offers a silent example for his own incipient madness:

> Thou sayest the King grows mad; I'll tell thee, friend,
> I am almost mad myself. I had a son,
> Now outlawed from my blood; he sought my life,
> But lately, very late. I loved him, friend,
> No father his son dearer. True to tell thee,
> The grief hath crazed my wits. (3.4.161–66)

Of course, Gloucester doesn't recognize Poor Tom as his son Edgar, but Edgar will play a very significant role in restoring Gloucester from his bitter despair and his wish for suicide. This is similar to the role Cordelia plays in recovering her father from his madness.

## Chapter Twenty-Five

# The Macbeths's Insomnia

The murders committed by Macbeth and Lady Macbeth produce the anxiety that denies them sleep, so that there is a sense in the play that they must continue murdering their enemies to try to sleep soundly. They need security in its literal sense of freedom from troubling care. But, of course, this security is illusory because they are deeply troubled by all of the murders, beginning with King Duncan.

The issue is raised most strongly right after the murder of the king. Macbeth is shaken by the fact that when one of the drunken grooms says "God bless us!" and the other "Amen," he, the murderer, "could not say 'Amen,'/ When they did say 'God bless us!'" (2.2.26, 28–29). He anxiously questions his wife: "But wherefore could not I pronounce 'Amen'? / I had most need of blessing, and "'Amen' / Stuck in my throat" (2.2.30–32). Macbeth cannot accept the fact that he is a murderer. Lady Macbeth's answers are totally unhelpful in this context: "Consider it not so deeply" (2.2.29) and "These deeds must not be thought / After these ways; so, it will make us mad" (2.2.32–33).

Macbeth cannot be comforted. He keeps repeating images of the sleep he and his wife will be forever denied:

> Methought I heard a voice cry, "Sleep no more!
> Macbeth does murder sleep"—the innocent sleep,
> Sleep that knits up the raveled [tangled] sleave of care,
> The death of each day's life, sore labor's bath,
> Balm of hurt minds, great nature's second course,
> Chief nourisher in life's feast— (2.2.34–39)

Lady Macbeth cuts off her husband's anguished apostrophes to a personified sleep and care with total incomprehension: "What do you mean?" (2.2.39).

125

But Macbeth cannot stop his lamentations: "Still it cried 'Sleep no more!' to all the house: / 'Glamis hath murdered sleep, and therefore Cawdor / Shall sleep no more: Macbeth shall sleep no more'" (2.2.40–42).

At this point in the play, there seems to be no way of reaching Lady Macbeth and convincing her that she is complicit in the murder of the king. She speaks in trivialities:

> Who was it that thus cried? Why, worthy thane,
> You do unbend your noble strength, to think
> So brainsickly of things. Go get some water,
> And wash this filthy witness from your hand. (2.2.43–46)

Macbeth is deeply troubled by the murder, and he cannot, of course, respond to his wife's impersonal remarks:

> Will all great Neptune's ocean wash this blood
> Clean from my hand? No; this my hand will rather
> The multitudinous seas incarnadine,
> Making the green one red. (2.2.59–62)

But Macbeth's cosmic images do not penetrate his wife's matter of factness. She still insists: "A little water clears us of this deed: / How easy is it then!" (2.2.66–67). It is interesting that Lady Macbeth is the one who, at the end of the play, goes mad with her unspoken grief.

Act 3, scene 2 is another crucial exposition of the sleep theme. Lady Macbeth seems to be requesting additional murders when she says:

> Nought's had, all's spent,
> Where our desire is got without content:
> 'Tis safer to be that which we destroy
> Than by destruction dwell in doubtful joy. (3.2.4–7)

Her mood has changed, but Macbeth is still in anguish. They can only sleep

> In the affliction of these terrible dreams
> That shake us nightly: better be with the dead,
> Whom we, to gain our peace, have sent to peace,
> Than on the torture of the mind to lie
> In restless ecstasy. (3.2.18–22)

"Ecstasy," a word describing the soul going out of the body, is often used by Shakespeare as a synonym for "madness," as in the four examples from *Hamlet.*

The scene ends with Macbeth's plan to kill Banquo and his son, Fleance, a dastardly act done, it seems, to put his wife in a better mood: "There's comfort yet; they are assailable. / Then be thou jocund" (3.2.39–40). Macbeth identifies himself with the powers of darkness in his final images:

> Light thickens, and the crow
> Makes wing to th' rooky wood
> Good things of day begin to droop and drowse,
> Whiles night's black agents to their preys do rouse. (3.2.50–53)

Macbeth is beginning to lose the sensitivity and anguish he had at the beginning of the play. He is now, without apology, one of night's black agents, proceeding to further murders.

The effects of the murders on Lady Macbeth are not felt until her sleepwalking scene in act 5, scene 1. Her insensitivity at the beginning of the play and her brooding sleeplessness finally culminate in her pitiful madness. A doctor and a gentlewoman are the observers in this scene. It is important to remember that Lady Macbeth is asleep throughout. Her mind is harrowed with guilt at the murder of the king, and she is continuously washing her hands to remove the blood stains: "Here's the smell of the blood still. All the perfumes of Arabia will not sweeten this little hand. Oh, oh, oh!" (5.1.52–54). This is very different from "A little water clears us of this deed" (2.2.66). In her madness, she mixes up details from earlier scenes. She assures her husband that the Ghost of Banquo will not reappear: "Wash your hands; put on your nightgown; look not so pale! I tell you yet again, Banquo's buried. He cannot come out on's grave" (5.1.64–66). Notice how preoccupied she is with going to bed and sleeping. Again, she seems to be speaking to an absent husband: "To bed, to bed! There's knocking at the gate. Come, come, come, come, give me your hand! What's done cannot be undone. To bed, to bed, to bed!" (5.1.68–71). The doctor says wisely: "More needs she the divine than the physician" (5.1.77). Presumably, Lady Macbeth dies at the frightening stage direction: "*A cry within of women*" (5.5.7 s.d.). In the final speech of the play, Malcolm reports that Macbeth's "fiendlike queen, / Who, as 'tis thought, by self and violent hands / Took off her life" (5.8.69–71).

It is interesting that the many speeches about sleeplessness in *Macbeth* seem to owe a debt to King Henry IV's long soliloquy in *2 Henry IV*. At the beginning of act 3, scene 1, the king enters "*in his nightgown, alone*" (3.1.1 s.d.) and speaks his formal apostrophe to sleep personified:

> O sleep, O gentle sleep,
> Nature's soft nurse, how have I frighted thee,
> That thou no more wilt weigh my eyelids down
> And steep my senses in forgetfulness? (3.1.5–8)

Henry muses on the fact that ordinary people sleep well: "O thou dull god, why li'st thou with the vile / In loathsome beds, and leavest the kindly couch / A watchcase [sentry box] or a common 'larum-bell?" (3.1.15–17). The king expatiates on the difference in the ability to sleep between nobles and commoners:

> Canst thou, O partial sleep, give thy repose
> To the wet sea-son in an hour so rude,
> And in the calmest and most stillest night,
> With all appliances and means to boot,
> Deny it to a king? (3.1.26–30)

The obvious answer lies in the king's conclusion: "Uneasy lies the head that wears a crown" (3.1.31). We remember that the king's conscience bothers him for the way he came to the throne: by deposing Richard II and having him murdered in the Tower. Macbeth and Lady Macbeth cannot forget about the deliberate murders that brought them to the throne of Scotland and the additional murders that were done to secure their kingship. Insomnia is a product of guilt, which nothing can assuage.

## Chapter Twenty-Six

# Roman Values in
# *Antony and Cleopatra*

Critics are generally agreed about the symbolic contrast in *Antony and Cleo-patra* between the values of Egypt and Rome, but, since Antony winds up in Egypt with Cleopatra, there is generally much stronger emphasis on the representation of Egypt than of Rome. This tends to skew the tragic conflict, especially in Antony. He is sure that he "must from this enchanting queen break off" (1.2.129) and "These strong Egyptian fetters I must break / Or lose myself in dotage" (1.2.117–18). "Dotage" is a strong word, signifying a foolish overfondness. Antony, the Roman triumvir and successful general, is never under any illusion that he will achieve a rhapsodic climax to his career by going back to Cleopatra. He knows that he is fated for a tragic end in Egypt, that he will lose his positive identity as a Roman. To be a Roman was popularly understood in terms of Stoic values: self-control, a strong sense of duty, seriousness of purpose, and an ability to rise above the petty misfor-tunes of daily life. Shakespeare's Romans generally seem to disregard the Stoic prohibition against suicide. It is nobler to die by one's own hand than to be led by one's captor in his triumphal procession. Cleopatra certainly seeks to avoid an ignoble end by dying "after the high Roman fashion" (4.15.90).

We should take these issues about Antony's tragedy more seriously than critics generally do. The matter is clearly laid out in the first speeches of the play. Philo, an officer in Antony's army, states the problem baldly:

> Nay, but this dotage of our general's
> O'erflows the measure. Those his goodly eyes
> That o'er the files and musters of the war
> Have glowed like plated Mars, now bend, now turn
> The office and devotion of their view

Upon a tawny front. (1.1.1–6)

"Dotage" is a strongly negative word for foolishness and excessive fondness, especially in love. To dote is a characteristic activity of older men. Antony's "captain's heart" has "become the bellows and the fan / To cool a gypsy's lust" (1.1.6, 9–10). Afterward, we see this speech enacted in the stage direction for the entrance of Antony, Cleopatra, her ladies, and her train "*with Eunuchs fanning her*" (1.1.10 s.d.). We are meant to understand that what Philo is speaking about is right there for everyone to see: that the great general Antony, the Triumvir of the Roman Empire, has lost his manhood in Egypt. The scene ends with Philo and his companion, Demetrius, speaking disparagingly about Antony's decline.

In the next scene, we see Antony preparing to return to Rome. Cleopatra puts the conflict succinctly: "He was disposed to mirth; but on the sudden / A Roman thought hath struck him" (1.2.83–84). A Roman thought is a serious thought, a manly thought as opposed to the time-dishonoring mirth of Egypt. The messenger from Rome delivers his bad news about how military affairs stand, and Antony is convinced that "These strong Egyptian fetters I must break / Or lose myself in dotage" (1.2.117–18). Antony is never in doubt about how things stand with him. His clarity is important for establishing a moral center in the play: "I must from this enchanting queen break off: / Ten thousand harms, more than the ills I know, / My idleness doth hatch" (1.2.129–31). "Enchanting" is a word associated with magic, as is the word "charm." Antony calls Cleopatra his "charm," or witch, twice in act 4, scene 12. He has no illusions about her: "She is cunning past man's thought" and "Would I had never seen her!" (1.2.146, 153). The "business" (1.2.172–73) of the Roman Empire cannot endure Antony's absence.

Act 1, scene 4 is the first scene set in Rome. Caesar disparages the present Antony, who "is not more manlike / Than Cleopatra" (1.4.5–6). To be manly is essential for a Roman soldier; it is the essence of what it means to be Roman. Remember how Lady Macbeth faults her husband for his lack of manliness when he sees the Ghost of Banquo. But Caesar also reminds us of Antony as he once was, the brave and heroic Roman soldier. It is interesting how deeply Caesar's account is steeped in the appetitive imagery of food and eating:

> When thou once
> Was beaten from Modena, where thou slew'st
> Hirtius and Pansa, consuls, at thy heel
> Did famine follow, whom thou fought'st against
> (Though daintily brought up) with patience more
> Than savages could suffer. Thou didst drink
> The stale [urine] of horses and the gilded puddle
> Which beasts would cough at. (1.4.56–63)

Caesar's admiration for Antony as he once was is unbounded:

> Thy palate then did deign
> The roughest berry on the rudest hedge.
> Yea, like the stag when snow the pasture sheets,
> The barks of trees thou browsed. On the Alps
> It is reported thou didst eat strange flesh,
> Which some did die to look on. (1.4.63–68)

All this detail about eating is necessary to show Antony's former fortitude. For Caesar, the images he evokes should be sufficient to persuade Antony to "Leave thy lascivious wassails" (1.4.56).

Antony's marriage to Octavia, Caesar's sister, marks his return to Rome and his attempted reconciliation with Caesar. But Enobarbus's description of Cleopatra's first meeting with Antony in her magnificent barge on the river Cydnus assures us that Octavia can never hope to restrain Antony from returning to Egypt. Maecenas says naively: "Now Antony must leave her utterly" (2.2.235), but Enobarbus is sure that "Never; he will not: / Age cannot wither her, nor custom stale / Her infinite variety" (2.2.236–38). Octavia's "beauty, wisdom, modesty" (2.2.243) may be a "blessèd lottery" (2.2.245), or prize won by lot, to Antony, but she cannot keep him.

Enobarbus's description of Octavia is conclusive: she is "of a holy, cold, and still conversation" (2.6.122–23), the very opposite of Cleopatra. The images that Caesar uses for his sister also make it certain that Antony will leave her:

> Most noble Antony,
> Let not the piece of virtue which is set
> Betwixt us as the cement of our love
> To keep it builded, be the ram to batter
> The fortress of it. (3.2.27–31)

These are all hard, material, Roman objects: cement, the battering ram, the fortress, not likely to capture Antony's heart.

The sequence is concluded by the messenger Cleopatra sends to describe her rival, who is "Dull of tongue, and dwarfish" (3.3.19). Of her gait, the report is that

> She creeps:
> Her motion and her station are as one.
> She shows a body rather than a life.
> A statue than a breather. (3.3.21–24)

In other words, Octavia is not at all lively or animated the way Cleopatra is. She is a lifeless statue rather than a living, breathing woman, which is the way that Caesar might have described his sister, as a perfectly passive but stately Roman matron. Late in the play, before her suicide, Cleopatra declares that she will not be taken captive to be "chastised with the sober eye / Of dull Octavia" (5.2.54–55).

Once Antony has returned to Egypt, his fortunes as a Roman soldier steadily decline. He loses the first sea battle with Caesar because he follows Cleopatra's ships in fleeing. He is "The noble ruin of her magic" (3.10.18): "Experience, manhood, honor, ne'er before / Did violate so itself" (3.10.22–23). Experience, manhood, honor are at the heart of what it means to be a Roman. Antony is aware that he has "lost command" (3.11.23). Like Cassio in *Othello*, he has "offended reputation, / A most unnoble swerving" (3.11.49–50). In a much repeated image, Antony speaks of his "sword, made weak by my affection" (3.11.67). He is self-condemned and he has lost any way of returning to Roman virtues.

Antony has not yet given up. He prepares for the second battle—which he wins—and resolves to "have one other gaudy [celebratory] night" (3.13.183). In act 4, scene 4 we see him putting on his armor with the help of his servant Eros. But Cleopatra wants to help too, and, in her tentative attempts, we see the conflict of Egypt and Rome enacted on stage:

*Cleopatra.* Nay, I'll help too.

What's this for?

*Antony.* Ah, let be, let be! Thou art

The armorer of my heart. False, false; this, this.

*Cleopatra.* Sooth, la, I'll help: thus it must be. (4.4.5–8)

This is all wonderfully colloquial and demonstrative. Antony appreciates what Cleopatra is doing: "Thou fumblest, Eros, and my queen's a squire / More tight at this than thou" (3.13.14–15). Antony has a moment of elation in which he seeks to demonstrate to Cleopatra his "royal occupation" (3.13.17).

But it is only a temporary illusion. After the loss of the crucial sea battle of Actium, Antony as a Roman soldier seems to dissolve. In a lyrical speech that is echoed in Prospero's revels speech in *The Tempest* (4.1), Antony loses his identity: "That which is now a horse, even with a thought / The rack dislimns, and makes it indistinct / As water is in water" (4.14.9–11). "Dislimns" is a coinage of Shakespeare, the opposite of "limns" meaning "paints." Antony cannot "hold this visible shape" (4.14.14) because Cleopatra has robbed him of his "sword" (4.14.23), an important symbol of his Roman self. He now, with the help of Eros, disarms:

Off, pluck off:
The sevenfold shield of Ajax cannot keep
The battery [beating] from my heart. O, cleave, my sides!
Heart, once be stronger than thy continent,
Crack thy frail case! Apace, Eros, apace.
No more a soldier. Bruisèd pieces, go;
You have been nobly borne. (4.14.37–43)

This is an important moment for Antony. He resolves to commit suicide with the help of Eros, but Eros kills himself instead. Antony does fall on his sword, but only wounds himself. He seeks in vain for someone to give him "Sufficing strokes for death" (4.14.116). He is now a pitiful, wounded figure. In the next scene, however, in Cleopatra's monument, Antony will die nobly: "a Roman, by a Roman / Valiantly vanquished" (4.15.57–58).

There is one further scene we should consider: act 4, scene 3, in which the god Hercules, Antony's tutelary deity, forsakes him. It is a strange, allegorical scene, with Antony's soldiers in all four corners of the stage. They hear "*Music of the hautboys [oboes] is under the stage*" (4.3.11 s.d.). It is a bad sign for the fortunes of Antony. As the Second Soldier says: "'Tis the god Hercules, whom Antony loved, / Now leaves him" (4.3.15–16).

Act 4, scene 3 echoes what we have already learned from the Soothsayer in act 2, scene 3. Next to Caesar, Antony is always unlucky. The Soothsayer advises him:

Therefore, O Antony, stay not by his side.
Thy daemon [guardian deity, like Hercules], that thy spirit which keeps thee, is
Noble, courageous, high, unmatchable,
Where Caesar's is not. But near him thy angel
Becomes afeard, as being o'erpow'red: therefore
Make space enough between you. (2.3.17–22)

This makes Antony's fall inevitable, as if it were willed by the gods. The Soothsayer is specific in his warning: "If thou dost play with him at any game, / Thou art sure to lose; and of that natural luck / He beats thee 'gainst the odds" (2.3.24–26). Antony agrees, but he is determined to abandon Octavia and go to Egypt: "And though I make this marriage for my peace, / I' th' East my pleasure lies" (2.3.38–39). So Antony knowingly goes to his doom.

# Chapter Twenty-Seven

# The Cultivation of Excess
# in *Timon of Athens*

This is an unusual play, probably written after Shakespeare's major tragedies but reflecting their influence. It is a bitter play, full of invective about money and ingratitude—a favorite, by its subject, of Karl Marx. The first scene sets out a kind of allegory that will show us Timon in prosperity, enjoying to the fullest extent his bounty, then the last two acts, Timon in adversity, self-banished from Athens and digging for roots in the forest, where he, ironically, finds an unlimited supply of gold. The play has recently been thought to be a collaborative effort of Shakespeare and Thomas Middleton, but it is problematic to establish who wrote what, so I will assume that it is all by Shakespeare.

In the long first scene, Timon is besieged by suitors seeking his patronage. We begin with a poet, a painter, a jeweler, and a merchant, who display or speak at length about their wares. It is a commercial introduction to the play. The Poet is probably the most important of the suitors. He begins by celebrating Timon's "Magic of bounty" (1.1.6), which has wide powers to attract: "all these spirits thy power / Hath conjured to attend" (1.1.6–7). All the persons seeking to receive Timon's rewards express fulsome flattery for their master.

The Poet, in commenting on the Painter's portrait of Timon, is excessive in his praise:

> Admirable. How this grace
> Speaks his own standing! What a mental power
> This eye shoots forth! How big imagination
> Moves in this lip! To th' dumbness of the gesture
> One might interpret. (1.1.30–34)

Of course, the audience in the theater sees the painting, which is obviously not the masterpiece the Poet is describing. So the initial feeling in *Timon* is one of hucksterism, of persons offering things for Timon to buy. The entrance to Timon's house is like a marketplace. All four of the suitors are full of pretense, and their pretentious language is associated with artists, or pretend artists. The Poet is the worst in speaking an abstract "artspeak." For his conclusion, he says of the painting: "It tutors nature; artificial strife / Lives in these touches, livelier than life" (1.1.37–38).

The Poet elaborates on his own poem, with disclaimers: "A thing slipped idly from me. / Our poesy is as a gum, which oozes / From whence 'tis nourished" (1.1.20–22). The Poet is so carried away by self-love that he doesn't seem to realize how unappealing a gum-like, oozing poetry is to his auditors. His poem is an allegory of the fickle goddess Fortuna, and it uncannily predicts the action of Shakespeare's play:

> I have upon a high and pleasant hill
> Feigned Fortune to be throned. The base o' th' mount
> Is ranked with all deserts, all kind of natures
> That labor on the bosom of this sphere
> To propagate their states. (1.1.63–67)

Fortune, "with her ivory hand, wafts" (1.1.70) Lord Timon to her.

But the goddess Fortuna cannot be trusted, and Timon is not secure on the top of Fortune's wheel:

> When Fortune in her shift and change of mood
> Spurns down her late beloved, all his dependants
> Which labored after him to the mountain's top,
> Even on their knees and hands, let him slip down,
> Not one accompanying his declining foot. (1.1.84–88)

It is surprising that the sycophantic Poet doesn't realize that this conclusion cannot be flattering to Timon—if he ever reads his special poem, which is doubtful.

The lordly Timon doesn't appear until line 94. He enters grandly, "*addressing himself courteously to every suitor*" (1.1.94 s.d.). He is like a preoccupied chairman of the board (a hint that has been picked up in many modern productions). He ardently desires that everyone love him, so that his bounty (a much repeated word) is showy and impersonal. He wants everyone to be his friend, another much repeated word in these early scenes. He overdoes it in a wild excess of generosity: "'Tis not enough to help the feeble up, / But to support him after" (1.1.107–8). The Poet, the Painter, and the Jeweler are all well rewarded, with Timon hardly regarding what is offered him. As he says to the Painter: "I like your work, / And you shall find I like it. Wait attendance / Till you hear further from me" (1.1.160–62). It is all so casual and so unexamined.

The entrance of the Cynic philosopher Apemantus offers a moral commentary on Timon's folly. Apemantus may be at the moral center of the play, but, like Thersites in *Troilus and Cressida*, whom he resembles, he is rude, scurrilous, and generally unattractive. He is the unpleasant, even despicable, truth-speaker, a character Shakespeare seemed to be fond of (compare Jaques in *Twelfth Night*). When Timon graciously asks him to dine, he refuses:

*Apemantus.* No. I eat not lords.

*Timon.* And [if] thou shouldst, thou'dst anger ladies.

*Apemantus.* O they eat lords; so they come by great bellies.

*Timon.* That's a lascivious apprehension. (1.1.206–10)

So the imagery is both cannibalistic and bawdy, a combination that runs throughout the play. Apemantus has a series of moralistic apothegms, which have no effect on Timon, who takes them as pure invective. For example: "He that loves to be flattered is worthy o' th' flatterer" (1.1.230–31), "Traffic's [trade's] thy god, and thy god confound thee" (1.1.244–45), and "The strain of man's bred out / Into baboon and monkey" (1.1.256–57).

The second scene of act 1 continues the unstoppable excess of Timon. He refuses repayment of his loan by Ventidius, who has suddenly become rich:

O by no means,
Honest Ventidius. You mistake my love;
I gave it freely ever, and there's none
Can truly say he gives, if he receives. (1.28–11)

Timon is preoccupied with dispensing unlimited love, friendship, generosity—call it what name you please. Repayment would only diminish his endeavor. Apemantus repeats his cannibalistic imagery: "O you gods! What a number of men eats Timon, and he sees 'em not! It grieves me to see so many dip their meat in one man's blood, and all the madness is, he cheers them up too" (1.2.38–42).

The entrance of Flavius, Timon's steward, strikes the first discordant note. In a long aside, Flavius assures us that Timon is bankrupt and that his exaggerated giving is a fantasy, based on unpayable loans: "He commands us to provide, and give great gifts, / And all out of an empty coffer" (1.2.195–96). But, unlike Apemantus, Flavius is sympathetic: "I bleed inwardly for my lord" (1.2.207). The climax of Timon's folly is spoken by an unnamed senator in the next scene:

If I want gold, steal but a beggar's dog
And give it Timon—why the dog coins gold.
If I would sell my horse and buy twenty moe
Better than he—why give the horse to Timon;
Ask nothing, give it him, it foals me straight,
And able horses. (2.1.5–10)

It is abundantly clear that Timon cannot maintain his histrionic image. In three wonderfully colloquial scenes (3.1–3), Timon's so-called friends cannot lend him anything. Lucullus even comments negatively on Timon's foolish honesty: "Every man has his fault, and honesty is his. I ha' told him on't, but I could ne'er get him from't" (3.1.28–30).

Timon leaves Athens and takes to the woods in a self-imposed exile. In the last two acts of the play, Timon digs for roots but discovers an unlimited supply of gold. By this convenient irony, we are brought back to the beginning of the play and the fact that money is at the root of all evil—a medieval moral apothegm. We can see why Karl Marx was so attached to the cash nexus of this play. The degree of excess is perhaps even greater in the last two acts of the play as Timon launches his vitriolic and misanthropic tirades against mankind. In act 5, scene 1, the Poet and the Painter reappear. They are the same grasping suitors as they were in act 1, but they think that Timon is only feigning poverty to test his beneficiaries. With utter cynicism, the Painter confides in the Poet: "Therefore 'tis not amiss we tender our loves to him in this supposed distress of his. It will show honestly in us, and is very likely to load our purposes with what they travail for, if it be a just and true report that goes of his having" (5.1.12–17). They have nothing in hand to show Timon, but the Painter is convinced that they can gain their rich rewards without having to produce anything: "Promising is the very air o' th' time; it opens the eyes of expectation. Performance is ever the duller for his act, and but in the plainer and simpler kind of people, the deed of saying is quite out of use" (5.1.23–27). The degree of corruption in the Poet and Painter has increased markedly since the beginning of the play.

With Alcibiades's whores in act 4, scene 3, Timon finds the perfect subject for his uncontrolled invective. Phrynia and Timandra are tough-talking street people who give as good as they get, provided that Timon gives them gold. Timon lectures Timandra about how to destroy mankind:

Be a whore still; they love thee not that use thee.
Give them diseases, leaving with thee their lust.
Make use of thy salt hours. Season the slaves
For tubs and baths; bring down rose-cheeked youth
To the tub-fast and the diet. (4.3.84–88)

Timon's discourse is so full of references to venereal disease and its supposed cure that biographically inclined critics have assumed that Shakespeare must have had syphilis at this point in his career. Phrynia and Timandra pretend to listen carefully to Timon's useful advice, but they have only one refrain, which they speak together: "Well, more gold. What then? / Believe't that we'll do anything for gold" (4.3.150–51) and "More counsel with more money, bounteous Timon" (4.3.168–69).

Timon's most significant exchanges are with Apemantus, who, like him, is also a rude misanthrope. Apemantus's first words are in fact a rebuke: "Men report / Thou dost affect my manners, and dost use them" (4.3.199–200). Apemantus assumes that Timon is only acting a part that he is not comfortable with: "The middle of humanity thou never knewest, but the extremity of both ends. When thou wast in thy gilt and thy perfume, they mocked thee for too much curiosity; in thy rags thou know'st none, but art despised for the contrary" (4.3.299–303). Apemantus speaks wisely but bitterly. He understands Timon as a misanthrope modeled on himself: "Thou hast cast away thyself, being like thyself: / A madman so long, now a fool" (4.3.221–22) and "Thou'dst courtier be again / Wert thou not beggar" (4.3.242–43). Of course, neither Timon nor Apemantus has any effect on each other, but Timon does pick up the suggestion that it is time for him to die.

The one saving note in this scene is Flavius, Timon's steward, who remains true to his master in adversity. He sympathizes with Timon in his fall: "What an alteration of honor has desp'rate want made! / What vilder thing upon the earth than friends, / Who can bring noblest minds to basest ends!" (4.3.464–66). He forces Timon to acknowledge that all of mankind is not hateful:

> Forgive my general and exceptless rashness,
> You perpetual-sober gods. I do proclaim
> One honest man. Mistake me not, but one.
> No more I pray—and he's a steward.
> How fain would I have hated all mankind,
> And thou redeem'st thyself. But all save thee
> I fell with curses. (4.3.498–504)

But Timon seems uncomfortable with Flavius, who has driven him out of his absolute misanthropy. He is eager to corrupt him with gold so that he will be like himself:

> Hate all, curse all, show charity to none,
> But let the famished flesh slide from the bone
> Ere thou relieve the beggar. Give to dogs
> What thou deniest to men. (4.3.530–33)

Timon's excessive invective seems particularly futile at this point. It is mere rhetoric, with no effect on Flavius. Again, the only thing Timon can profitably do now is prepare to die.

## Chapter Twenty-Eight

# Coriolanus's Manliness

Coriolanus is represented as a Roman warrior in the play that bears his name. He is like other military protagonists in Shakespeare, such as Henry V and Macbeth. In fact, Coriolanus owes something to the way manliness is defined in the Ghost of Banquo scene in *Macbeth* (3.4). In *King Lear*, when Edmund sends a captain to kill Lear and Cordelia in prison, the captain agrees by saying only: "I cannot draw a cart, nor eat dried oats. / If it be man's work, I'll do't" (5.3.39–40). Killing is defined as a male function. We often see Coriolanus engaged in bloody combat, which is, of course, praiseworthy although represented savagely.

Act 1, scene 4 shows us Caius Marcius—he will be called Coriolanus afterward—fighting the Volscians before the city of Corioli. Marcius prays to Mars, the god of war, to "make us quick in work, / That we with smoking swords may march from hence" (1.4.10–11). The swords will be smoking with the blood of the enemy. After Marcius is shut in the gates of the city, everyone applauds his heroism. It is truly astounding: "He is himself alone, / To answer all the city" (1.4.51–52). The Romans assume he will be killed, but we see him suddenly come on stage *"bleeding, assaulted by the enemy"* (1.4.62 s.d.). He appears again "as he were flayed" (1.6.22). So Marcius's bloody wounds are a sign of his Roman valor. After the battle, he receives the honorific name of Coriolanus.

The Roman commander Cominius describes Coriolanus's military career: "At sixteen years, / When Tarquin made a head for Rome, he fought / Beyond the mark of others" (2.2.87–89). Cominius celebrates Coriolanus's young feats of valor: "His pupil age / Man-ent'red thus, he waxèd like a sea" (2.2.98–99). In the present battle for Corioles:

His sword, death's stamp,

Where it did mark, it took; from face to foot
He was a thing of blood, whose every motion
Was timed with dying cries. (2.2.107–10)

This is superlative praise for Coriolanus as a military hero.

Cominius's description is bolstered by what Volumnia says of her son. The imagery is still of blood and wounds as a symbol of Coriolanus's indomitable courage.

In a peaceful domestic scene (1.3), Volumnia cannot help boasting of how her son proves himself a man. Virgilia, Marcius's tender-hearted wife, may be horrified by her mother-in-law, but Volumnia is not to be restrained in her account of her son's honor: "had I a dozen sons, each in my love alike, and none less dear than thine and my good Marcius, I had rather had eleven die nobly for their country than one voluptuously surfeit out of action" (1.3.20–25). When Virgilia objects strenuously to Volumnia's mention of Marcius's "bloody brow," the mother replies with vigorous contempt:

Away, you fool! It more becomes a man
Than gilt his trophy. The breasts of Hecuba,
When she did suckle Hector, looked not lovelier
Than Hector's forehead when it spit forth blood
At Grecian sword, contemning. (1.3.39–43)

This echoes the cruel imagery of Lady Macbeth's "unsex me" soliloquy (1.5.42f). Lady Valeria's account of how Marcius's son caught a gilded butterfly and cruelly tore it to pieces ("mammocked it") (1.3.60–65) is in the same noble warrior spirit as Volumnia's boasting of her son.

After the battle of Corioles, again there is a conflict between Virgilia and Volumnia. Coriolanus's mother is, perversely, glad to hear that her son is wounded: "I thank the gods for't" (2.1.124). She considers his wounds as badges of honor and boasts that "He had before this last expedition twenty-five wounds upon him" (2.1.157–58). The wounds figure importantly in Coriolanus's standing for consul in the gown of humility. Volumnia's exaggerated praise is for her son as a kind of killing machine: "Before him he carries noise, and behind him he leaves tears. Death, that dark spirit, in's nervy [sinewy] arm doth lie, Which, being advanced, declines, and then men die" (2.1.162–65).

These kinds of bold statements don't do much to advance a humanistic view of Coriolanus, but we have to acknowledge that the play is rabidly anti-democratic, praising the virtues of war with a kind of fierce energy. This doesn't, of course, mean that Shakespeare identifies with the values of Coriolanus.

There is abundant irony in act 3, scene 2, when Volumnia schools her son on how to be politic and to gain the consulship by deceit. Because she is herself in her support of patrician values, it is odd to hear her tell her son that he is "too absolute" (3.2.39). She instructs him in the false role he has to play to the Roman citizens—as if he were an actor in the theater:

> Go to them with this bonnet in thy hand;
> And thus far having stretched it (here be with them),
> Thy knee bussing the stones (for in such business
> Action is eloquence, and the eyes of th' ignorant
> More learnèd than the ears), waving thy head,
> Which often thus correcting thy stout heart,
> Now humble as the ripest mulberry
> That will not hold the handling. (3.2.73–80)

This is an extraordinary speech, since Volumnia is expounding a doctrine that she doesn't believe in. We applaud Coriolanus's honest repulsion against the dishonesty of playing politic: "Would you have me / False to my nature? Rather say I play / The man I am" (3.2.14–16). This is an important part of Coriolanus's manliness: to be true to himself.

# Chapter Twenty-Nine

# The Saintly Marina in *Pericles*

Although *Pericles* is probably a collaboration, the scenes with Marina, Pericles's daughter, from acts 4 and 5 are generally thought to be by Shakespeare. Marina is a super-romantic heroine, like Perdita, Imogen, and Miranda in her innocence, but going beyond them in a feeling that she is also saintly. There is a good deal of religious vocabulary used for her. For example, in act 4, scene 5, two gentlemen coming from the brothel in Mytilene comment on her ability to convert the lewd patrons to an unlooked-for chastity. The First Gentleman says: "But to have divinity preached there! Did you ever dream of such a thing?" (4.5.4–5). And at the end of the scene, the First Gentleman says again: "I'll do anything now that is virtuous; but I am out of the road of rutting [copulating] forever" (4.5.8–9).

In act 4, scene 6, Marina converts Lysimachus, governor of Mytilene, to chastity. As the Bawd says at the beginning of the scene, "She's able to freeze the god Priapus" and "she would make a puritan of the devil, if he should cheapen [buy] a kiss of her" (4.5.3–4, 9–10). Lysimachus cannot resist her preaching: "Persever in that clear way thou goest, / And the gods strengthen thee!" (4.5.111–12). Marina is constantly invoking the gods, and even Boult cannot refuse her "holy words" (4.5.138). She is a liability in the brothel, as the Pander and his wife recognize. It is an interesting aspect of *Pericles* that this is Shakespeare's most sexually explicit play, going beyond the deeds of Mistress Overdone and Pompey in *Measure for Measure*, yet the actions of its heroine in the brothel seem like a saint's life, especially in her easy converting of all of the patrons—and Boult, too.

Much about Marina is presented as miraculous. For example, just as Leonine is about to murder her, she is suddenly rescued by pirates (4.1), which recalls Hamlet's being rescued by pirates as he is being sent to his

145

death in England (4.6). In act 5, scene 1, Pericles describes her attraction in relation to his wife, Thaisa, whom he believes has perished at sea:

> My dearest wife was like this maid, and such
> My daughter might have been: my queen's square brows;
> Her stature to an inch; as wandlike straight;
> As silver-voiced; her eyes as jewel-like
> And cased [enclosed] as richly; in pace another Juno;
> Who starves the ears she feeds, and makes them hungry
> The more she gives them speech. (5.1.110–16)

This echoes a line in *Antony and Cleopatra* in which Enobarbus says that Cleopatra "makes hungry / Where most she satisfies" (2.2.239–40).

We first see Marina in act 3, scene 3, as Lychorida, her nurse, enters with the baby in her arms. In act 4, scene 1, Marina, like Perdita in *The Winter's Tale*, enters with a basket of flowers to strew on Lychorida's grave:

> the yellows, blues,
> The purple violets, and marigolds,
> Shall as a carpet hang upon thy grave,
> While summer days doth last. (4.1.14–17)

Marina already seems a pitiable creature just as Dionyza and Cleon are plotting to kill her:

> Ay me, poor maid,
> Born in a tempest, when my mother died,
> This world to me is as a lasting storm,
> Whirring me from my friends. (4.1.17–20)

In the style of contemporary romances, she is rescued by pirates from Leonine, only to be sold into slavery.

In the brothel, Marina doesn't accuse anyone of injustice but bears her plight resignedly. Boult boasts that "thunder shall not so awake the beds of eels as my giving out her beauty stirs up the lewdly inclined" (4.2.144–46). But this sexual talk has no effect on Marina, who seems to have no doubt of preserving her virginity: "If fires be hot, knives sharp, or waters deep, / Untied I still my virgin knot will keep" (4.2.149–50). She appeals to the goddess Diana to aid her in her purpose, and Diana does appear to Pericles in a dream (at 5.1.242). It is interesting how many echoes there are in *Pericles* of other plays of Shakespeare. In this context we anticipate Prospero's concern with Miranda's "virgin-knot" in *The Tempest* (4.1.15).

In act 5, scene 1, Gower as Chorus (like the Choruses in *Henry V*) predicts the miraculous effect Marina will have on her grieving father by describing her goddess-like work in Mytilene outside the brothel:

> She sings like one immortal, and she dances
> As goddesslike to her admired lays;
> Deep clerks she dumbs, and with her neele [needle] composes
> Nature's own shape of bud, bird, branch, or berry,
> That even her art sisters [is like] the natural roses;
> Her inkle [linen thread], silk, twin with the rubied cherry. (5.0.3–8)

So we are sure that her mourning father, *"unkempt and clad in sackcloth"* (5.1.1 s.d.), will be recovered from his deep depression.

This moving scene (5.1) resembles the end of *The Winter's Tale*, where the supposed statue of Hermione, carved by Julio Romano, is brought back to life. All of Shakespeare's late romances, especially *Pericles*, emphasize effects of wonder and the marvelous. In this play (and in the statue scene of *The Winter's Tale*), music plays an important role. Marina begins by singing to her disconsolate father, but the recognition proceeds slowly. Pericles seems to feel that Marina resembles his supposedly dead wife, Thaisa: "thou lookest / Like one I loved indeed" (5.1.128–29). Echoing a line from *Twelfth Night*, the grieving father says: "yet thou dost look / Like Patience gazing on kings' graves, and smiling / Extremity out of act" (5.1.141–43). In *Twelfth Night*, Viola, in love with Duke Orsino, speaks of her imaginary sister sitting "like Patience on a monument, / Smiling at grief" (2.4.114–15). Patience is, presumably, a figure carved on a tomb.

Bit by bit, the recognition scene proceeds, until Pericles is about to burst with "this great sea of joys rushing upon me," which may "drown me with their sweetness" (5.1.196, 198). He finally realizes a triumphant rebirth: "O, come hither, / Thou that beget'st him that did thee beget" (5.1.198–99). The high point of this scene is when Pericles hears the "music of the spheres" (5.1.232) that no else can hear: "I hear most heavenly music. / It nips me unto list'ning, and thick slumber / Hangs upon mine eyes" (5.1.236–38). It is at this moment that the goddess Diana appears to him in a dream and counsels him to do sacrifice "upon my altar" (5.1.244) and recount all his story. The romance of *Pericles* in itself is supposed to have a miraculous and revivifying effect.

## Chapter Thirty

# Imogen

### Romance Heroine
### *of* Cymbeline

Imogen is very different from the earlier heroines of Shakespeare's comedies, who were witty and satirical, like Beatrice in *Much Ado About Nothing* and Rosalind in *As You Like It*. Imogen is almost an ideal image of a pure and innocent young woman, without any discernible faults, like Perdita in *The Winter's Tale*, Miranda in *The Tempest*, and Marina in *Pericles*. They are all characters in Shakespeare's late romances. They are distinguished by their unlimited and often breathless devotion to their spouses, their lovers, or their fathers (as is the case with Marina). Adversity or rejection only increases the degree of their commitment.

Imogen's love of her new husband, Posthumus Leonatus, who is quickly exiled, is unbounded, as is her contempt for the suit of Cloten, the foolish son of the queen. Posthumus's ill-conceived wager with Iachimo in Rome on his wife's fidelity has unfortunate consequences, since it unleashes a flood of anti-feminist vituperation. Posthumus is too trusting because the villainous Iachimo intends to win his wager by whatever means it takes. With italianate cunning, he arranges to hide in a trunk in Imogen's bedchamber, where he can freely note the details of the scene, steal her bracelet (a gift from her husband—this echoes the motif of the handkerchief in *Othello*), and make lewd observations about her body. What infuriates Posthumus and convinces him of his wife's adultery is Iachimo's crowning detail:

> On her left breast
> A mole cinque-spotted [with five spots], like the crimson drops
> I' th' bottom of a cowslip. Here's a voucher

> Stronger than ever law could make. This secret
> Will force him think I have picked the lock and ta'en
> The treasure of her honor. (2.2.38–42)

What complicates Iachimo's role is that he seems to have fallen in love with Imogen at first sight, as he exclaims in an aside:

> All of her that is out of door [visible] most rich!
> If she be furnished with a mind so rare,
> She is alone th' Arabian bird [the phoenix], and I
> Have lost the wager. Boldness be my friend!
> Arm me, audacity. (1.6.15–19)

We get the impression that Imogen is so beautiful that even a dastardly schemer like Iachimo cannot help falling in love with her.

Imogen is related to Desdemona in *Othello* and Hermione in *The Winter's Tale*. All three are wives falsely accused by jealous husbands. Othello kills Desdemona, but Hermione and Imogen manage to survive and live happily ever after. But the jealousy and the erroneous assumption of infidelity create a strong current of antifeminine vituperation, especially in *Cymbeline*. Posthumus is so shocked by Iachimo's report that he has a soliloquy in act 2, scene 5, in which he adds his own disgusting sexual details to Iachimo's account:

> This yellow Iachimo in an hour, was't not?
> Or less? At first? Perchance he spoke not, but,
> Like a full-acorned boar, a German one,
> Cried "O!" and mounted. (2.5.14–17)

This leads directly to Posthumus's diatribe against women:

> Could I find out
> The woman's part in me! For there's no motion
> That tends to vice in man but I affirm
> It is the woman's part. Be it lying, note it,
> The woman's; flattering, hers; deceiving, hers;
> Lust and rank thoughts, hers, hers; revenges, hers;
> Ambitions, covetings, change of prides [excesses], disdain,
> Nice longing, slanders, mutability,
> All faults that have a name, nay, that hell knows,
> Why, hers, in part or all, but rather all. (2.5.19–28)

So Imogen, in the earlier part of the play, suffers slander through no fault of her own. Her dear and loyal husband is set against her; her father, King Cymbeline, disdains her marriage to Posthumus; and the queen wants to see her married to her foolish son Cloten.

Imogen recovers in our esteem in the third act, after Pisanio, Posthumus's servant, receives a letter from his master asking him to murder his faithless wife. But he doesn't reveal his letter at this point. Imogen is ecstatic that she too has received a letter from Posthumus, and she seems beside herself with joy even before she opens it:

> Let what is here contained relish of love,
> Of my lord's health, of his content—yet not
> That we two are asunder; let that grieve him . . .
> Good wax, thy leave. Blest be
> You bees that make these locks of counsel. (3.2.30–32, 35–36)

She is already blessing the bees that make the sealing wax that encloses the letter.

Once she learns from the letter that her husband is at Milford Haven, she anticipates seeing him with a breathlessness that is typical of the heroines of Shakespeare's late romances:

> Then, true Pisanio,
> Who long'st like me to see thy lord, who long'st—
> O, let me bate—but not like me, yet long'st,
> But in a fainter kind—O, not like me!
> For mine's beyond beyond: say, and speak thick—
> Love's counselor should fill the bores of hearing,
> To th' smothering of the sense—how far it is
> To this same blessèd Milford. (3.2.52–59)

Longing "beyond beyond"—if this is even imaginable, it takes Imogen an awfully long time to ask Pisanio how far it is to Milford Haven, but her absolute love overwhelms her ability to ask a direct question.

In act 3, scene 4, Pisanio finally lets her see the dire letter from her husband asking him to kill her. Imogen is devastated by this strange, slanderous letter, to which Pisanio says in pity: "What shall I need to draw my sword? The paper / Hath cut her throat already" (3.4.32–33). Her reaction is like that of Desdemona to Othello's accusations. She accepts the present reality, but her mournfulness is moving. She cannot imagine what is involved in being false to her husband:

> False to his bed? What is it to be false?
> To lie in watch [wakefulness] there and to think of him?
> To weep 'twixt clock and clock? If sleep charge [load] nature,
> To break it with a fearful dream of him
> And cry myself awake? That's false to's bed, is it? (3.4.40–44)

We commiserate with Imogen in her grief, as does Pisanio.

She longs for death and offers her own sword to Pisanio:

> Look,
> I draw the sword myself. Take it, and hit
> The innocent mansion of my love, my heart.
> Fear not, 'tis empty of all things but grief.
> Thy master is not there, who was indeed
> The riches of it. Do his bidding, strike! (3.4.66–71)

But Pisanio has only pity for the falsely accused Imogen, and he rescues her by an ingenious plot device: disguising her as a boy, Fidele, and reporting to his master that he has killed her.

The labyrinthine plot has Fidele meeting her real brothers, Guiderius and Arviragus (though not revealed at this point); supposedly dying from a potion prepared by Cornelius, the queen's physician (like that concocted by Friar Lawrence for Juliet in *Romeo and Juliet*); being buried with lyrical ceremony; mistaking Cloten's headless body for that of Posthumus; but, eventually, as a servant of Lucius, the Roman general, being restored, in the final scene of the play (5.5), to her father, King Cymbeline, and to her husband, Posthumus Leonatus. The mysterious oracle is fulfilled and the play ends happily.

# Chapter Thirty-One

# Speech Rhythms in
# *The Winter's Tale*

The blank verse in *The Winter's Tale* is different from the blank verse in Shakespeare's earlier comedies. It is much less regular in conforming to the five-beat, iambic pentameter line, which, according to the rules of scansion, consists of five iambs; in other words, five iambic feet (a sequence of five unstressed and stressed syllables). In Shakespeare's later comic romances like *The Winter's Tale*, dramatic speech rhythms override the iambic pattern (a regular succession of unstressed and stressed syllables), as if the characters urgently need to break out of it. The context demands many substitutions for the iambic foot. There is also a good deal of variation in the pauses, or caesuras, within the line. In a regular blank verse line, we expect only one pause in the middle, after the second or third foot. One other prosodic device we need to take account of is enjambment, or the continuation of a line beyond the five-beat limit onto the next line, which creates a feeling of extending the blank verse beyond the expected five beats, or five feet. The opposite of an enjambed line is an end-stopped line, which has a distinct pause after every five-feet line. In poetry (especially of the eighteenth century), end-stopped lines were in vogue, particularly end-stopped rhymed lines, which were called heroic couplets. In *The Winter's Tale*, we are interested in the way that dramatic speech plays against the regular five-beat, iambic pentameter pattern.

A good example of a characteristic speech of *The Winter's Tale* is Florizel's confession of his love for Perdita in the sheep-shearing scene:

> What you do
> Still betters what is done. When you speak, sweet,
> I'd have you do it ever; when you sing,

> I'd have you buy and sell so; so give alms,
> Pray so; and for the ord'ring your affairs,
> To sing them too. When you do dance, I wish you
> A wave o' th' sea, that you might ever do
> Nothing but that—move still, still so,
> And own no other function. Each your doing,
> So singular in each particular,
> Crowns what you are doing in the present deeds,
> That all your acts are queens. (4.4.135–46)

The only regular iambic pentameter line in this speech is 144: "So singular in each particular," but the internal rhyme of "singular" and "particular" tends to throw its regularity off. There are many substitutions for iambic feet (unstressed plus stressed syllables). "Pray so" in line 139 is a trochee (stressed plus unstressed syllable), "When you speak" in line 136 is an anapest (two unstressed plus a stressed syllable), and "Nothing but" in line 142 is a dactyl (stressed plus two unstressed syllables). Depending upon how one scans relative to the meaning, there are many spondees (two stressed syllables); for example, line 142 seems to have two spondees together in "move still, still so" (four stressed syllables). In other words, Florizel's speech makes for highly irregular blank verse. The verse form follows the emotional and dramatic necessities of what Florizel is expressing.

Since the lines have so many accented syllables, there are many unexpected pauses, or caesuras. In line 139, there is a distinct pause after the first foot: "Pray so." There are two distinct pauses in line 140: after the second foot ("To sing them too") and after the fourth foot ("When you do dance"). Line 142 has so many accents that it is difficult to place the pauses, but I think there is a caesura after the second foot ("Nothing but that") and after the fourth foot ("move still"). All of these so-called irregularities and substitutions in the blank verse line help to give Florizel's love speech its dramatic impact. The speech rhythm is charged with strong feeling that overrides our blank verse expectations.

We may also note that two lines are enjambed; in other words, the meaning is carried over into the next line. For example, line 140 is not end-stopped. "I wish you" at the end is continued in "A wave o' th' sea" in the next line. Similarly, line 141 continues over into line 142: "that you might ever do" needs "Nothing but that" to complete the sense of what Florizel is saying. This speech also uses other poetic devices such as alliteration, internal rhyme or half-rhyme, and repetition of key words to underscore its poetic meaning.

Let us take another example from this same context: Perdita's speech just before Florizel's in the sheep-shearing scene (4.4):

> O Proserpina,

For the flow'rs now, that, frighted, thou let'st fall
From Dis's wagon! Daffodils,
That come before the swallow dares, and take
The winds of March with beauty; violets, dim,
But sweeter than the lids of Juno's eyes,
Or Cytherea's breath; pale primroses,
That die unmarried ere they can behold
Bright Phoebus in his strength (a malady
Most incident to maids); bold oxlips, and
The crown imperial; lilies of all kinds,
The flower-de-luce being one. O, these I lack
To make you garlands of, and my sweet friend,
To strew him o'er and o'er! (4.4.116–29)

This speech tends to have mostly regular blank verse lines (except for line 118, which has only four feet). There are many caesuras, especially in line 117, which has three. The first is after the second foot, "For the flow'rs now," the second after "that," and the third after "frighted." Line 120 has two pauses, the first after "beauty," the second after "violets." In line 127 there is a caesura after "being one" and another after "O." Perdita's speech makes important use of enjambment to give it a sense of fluency in periods that extend beyond the end of the line. Line 117 continues into line 118: "thou let'st fall / From Dis's wagon," and so does line 119 go on to its conclusion in line 120: "and take / The winds of March with beauty." The description of "pale primroses" continues for two lines without an interruption in the meaning: "That die unmarried ere they can behold / Bright Phoebus in his strength (a malady / Most incident to maids)." One can see why Shakespeare manipulates the blank verse line to give Perdita an effect of lyrical sweetness and fluency. The unexpected caesuras and enjambment allow her to have a more natural speech rhythm.

There are many possible examples of the distinctive speech rhythms of *The Winter's Tale* as set against regular, iambic pentameter blank verse, but I shall restrict myself to two powerful examples from Leontes and Paulina. Toward the beginning of the play, the frantic quality of Leontes's jealousy is expressed in the distorted rhythms of his speech. In act 1, scene 2, he seems to be reasoning with Camillo about his wife's infidelity:

Is whispering nothing?
Is leaning cheek to cheek? Is meeting noses?
Kissing with inside lip? Stopping the career [running course]
Of laughter with a sigh (a note infallible
Of breaking honesty)? Horsing foot on foot?
Skulking in corners? Wishing clocks more swift?
Hours, minutes? Noon, midnight? And all eyes
Blind with the pin and web [cataract], but theirs; theirs only.

That would unseen be wicked? Is this nothing?
Why, then the world and all that's in't is nothing,
The covering sky is nothing. Bohemia nothing,
My wife is nothing, nor nothing have these nothings,
If this be nothing. (1.2.284–96)

The incantatory repetition of "nothing" sets a demented tone to Leontes's supposedly factual arguments. The insistent and urgent questions have the same effect, since they can hardly be based on Leontes's personal observations. The strong rhythm is established by substituting trochaic feet (stress plus unstressed syllables) for the expected iambs (unstressed plus stressed feet) in virtually every line. The word "nothing" is naturally a trochee, and it occurs nine times in this passage. Other trochaic feet are "noses" (285), "Kissing" (286), "Stopping" (286), "Horsing" (288), "Skulking" (289), "Wishing" (289), "Blind with" (291), and "theirs only" (291). There are probably more trochees, depending upon how one does the scansion. We should also note the two spondees (two stresses) in line 290: "Hours, minutes? Noon, midnight?"

There is also a good deal of enjambment. Three lines are run together in 286 to 288: "Stopping the career / Of laughter with a sigh (a note infallible / Of breaking honesty)?" This almost seems like prose rather than blank verse. Another three-line enjambment is 290 to 292: "And all eyes / Blind with the pin and web, but theirs; theirs only, / That would unseen be wicked?" The point of these substitutions for the regular iambic pentameter is to convey Leontes's disordered jealousy. There are strong emotions packed into Leontes's repeated accusations, and these are expressed by overriding the iambic pentameter pattern.

As a final example, I would like to look at Paulina's eloquent speech in the last scene of the play (5.3), where she directs the "statue" of Hermione to come down off its pedestal:

Music, awake her: strike.
'Tis time; descend; be stone no more; approach;
Strike all that look upon with marvel; come;
I'll fill your grave up. Stir; nay, come away;
Bequeath to death your numbness, for from him
Dear life redeems you. You perceive she stirs.
Start not; her actions shall be holy as
You hear my spell is lawful. Do not shun her
Until you see her die again, for then
You kill her double. Nay, present your hand.
When she was young, you wooed her; now, in age,
Is she become the suitor? (5.3.98–109)

This speech has a number of trochaic substitutions (stressed plus un-stressed syllables) for iambic feet (unstressed plus stressed syllables), especially in the imperatives that Paulina speaks to Leontes; for example, "Music" (98), "Strike" (100), "Bequeath" (102), and "Start" (104). But the speech is remarkable for the large number of pauses, or caesuras, which emphasize its dramatic quality. Line 99, for example, has three distinct pauses—after "time," "descend," and "more"—when we expect a typical blank verse line to have only a single caesura after the second or third foot. In other lines, the caesura comes late, after the fourth foot: after "marvel" in line 100, after "nay" in line 101, after "again" in line 106, and after "now" in line 108. In several lines, the caesura comes early, after the first foot: after "time" in line 99, and after "Start not" in line 104. This irregularity in the expected blank verse line endows what Paulina says with a strong speech rhythm.

There is also a good deal of enjambment to encourage the listeners or readers to think that they are not being burdened with the regular five-beat, end-stopped pattern. For example, line 102 continues into line 103: "for from him / Dear life redeems you." Line 104 extends to the next line: "shall be holy as / You hear my spell is lawful." Similarly, the meaning of line 105 is not completed until line 106: "Do not shun her / Until you see her die again," and line 106 needs line 107 to make its statement: "for then / You kill her double." These variations from the fixed iambic pentameter form heighten our sense of musical, dramatic speech.

# Chapter Thirty-Two

# Prospero's "Art" in
# *The Tempest*

Prospero is the only magician in Shakespeare, and magic—what Prospero calls his "art"—is very important in the play. The word is used at least ten times to refer to Prospero's white magic, what he has learned from careful study of books. Peter Greenaway's film version of the play is, in fact, called *Prospero's Books* (1991). Prospero definitely does not practice black magic. He makes no compact with the devil, as Doctor Faustus does in Marlowe's play. Nevertheless, there is a certain danger in Prospero's magic, which sets him apart from other mortals. At the end of the play, he forgives his enemies (like Duke Vincentio in *Measure for Measure*) and renounces his magical powers. This seems to be essential for him to resume his dukedom of Milan and, as it were, to rejoin the human race.

Let us look at some of the most important references to Prospero's art. In the long, expository scene of act 1, scene 2, Miranda speaks of her father's art in the first line of her first speech: "If by your art, my dearest father, you have / Put the wild waters in this roar, allay them" (1.2.1–2). The tempest that opens the play is only a show, a performance, like the wedding masque in act 4, scene 1. It was presented by Ariel, Prospero's attendant spirit, at his master's instructions. That is acknowledged in the question he asks Ariel: "Hast thou, spirit, / Performed, to point, the tempest that I bade thee?" (1.2.193–94).

He congratulates him: "Ariel, thy charge / Exactly is performed" (1.2.237–38). Later, Prospero is pleased with Ariel's role as harpy, who snatches away the banquet:

> Bravely the figure of this harpy hast thou
> Performed, my Ariel; a grace it had, devouring.

Of my instruction hast thou nothing bated
In what thou hadst to say. (3.3.83–86)

Prospero speaks like the director of a play, praising his actors for their performance. He uses the same words for Ariel's dealing with the conspiracy of Caliban, Trinculo, and Stephano: "Thou and thy meaner fellows your last service / Did worthily perform; and I must use you / In such another trick" (4.1.35–37).

The point of Prospero's art is to present illusions, performances, shows that effectively charm his adversaries. He uses his magic like a dramatist, directing his actors (principally Ariel) on how to realize his script. It is also purposive; for example, he prepares carefully for the wedding masque for Ferdinand and Miranda. It is an artistic product of his laborious, bookish study. As he says at the end of act 3, scene 1: "I'll to my book; / For yet ere suppertime must I perform / Much business appertaining" (3.1.94–96). And, as he says later:

I must
Bestow upon the eyes of this young couple
Some vanity of mine art. It is my promise,
And they expect it from me. (4.1.39–42)

Prospero seems proud of his playwriting skills, which he calls, offhandedly, "Some vanity of mine art." "Vanity" is used in the apologetic sense of a trifling illusion.

It is interesting that Prospero calls his conjuring robe his "art" in his speech to his daughter before he tells her the story of her previous life: "Lend thy hand / And pluck my magic garment from me. So. / Lie there my art" (1.2.23–25). Once he has taken off his "magic garment," he can proceed with his narrative as an ordinary mortal. He assures Miranda that the tempest was merely an illusion:

I have with such provision in mine art
So safely ordered that there is no soul—
No, not so much perdition as an hair
Betid to any creature in the vessel
Which thou heard'st cry, which thou saw'st sink. (1.2.28–32)

The good Gonzalo considers the preservation of all the passengers on the ship a "miracle"; moreover, the tempest seems to have laundered their clothes: "That our garments, being, as they were, drenched in the sea, hold, notwithstanding, their freshness and glosses, being rather new-dyed than stained with salt water" (2.1.64–67). This is exactly what the Boatswain reports at the end of the play:

our ship,
Which, but three glasses [hours] since, we gave out split,
Is tight and yare and bravely rigged as when
We first put out to sea. (5.1.222–25)

This is the proof of Prospero's natural magic, or theurgy, which is a neo-Platonic term for magic performed with the aid of beneficent spirits.

Prospero's art is nurtured by close study of books. Remember that one of Gonzalo's favors to the Duke of Milan when he was exiled by his usurping brother, Antonio, and set afloat was to provide him with books: "Knowing I loved my books, he furnished me / From mine own library with volumes that / I prize above my dukedom" (1.2.166–68). Prospero undoubtedly lost his dukedom because of his bookishness. As he explains to his daughter, he was

for the liberal arts
Without a parallel. Those being all my study,
The government I cast upon my brother
And to my state grew stranger, being transported
And rapt in secret studies. (1.2.73–77)

Presumably, "secret studies" means the study of magic, like Doctor Faustus.

At the end of his narration, before he puts Miranda to sleep (whether she will or not—is he using hypnotism?), he speaks of his studies as if they included astrology:

by my prescience
I find my zenith doth depend upon
A most auspicious star, whose influence
If now I court not, but omit, my fortunes
Will ever after droop. (1.2.180–84)

In *Romeo and Juliet*, the Prologue speaks of "A pair of star-crossed lovers" (1.0.6) and Romeo, before he takes his own life, vows to "shake the yoke of inauspicious stars / From this world-wearied flesh" (5.3.111–12). Prospero, like Brutus in *Julius Caesar*, must take the "tide in the affairs of men . . . at the flood" (4.3.215–16) or his fortunes will droop.

Prospero commands the spirit Ariel, reminding him how he freed him from imprisonment by the witch Sycorax, the mother of Caliban:

And, for thou wast a spirit too delicate
To act her earthy and abhorred commands,
Refusing her grand hests, she did confine thee,
By help of her more potent ministers,
And in her most unmitigable rage,
Into a cloven pine; within which rift
Imprisoned thou didst painfully remain

A dozen years; within which space she died
And left thee there, where thou didst vent thy groans
As fast as millwheels strike. (1.2.273–82)

By his superior knowledge of sorcery and witchcraft, Prospero comes to the rescue of Ariel: "It was my art, / When I arrived and heard thee, that made gape / The pine, and let thee out" (1.2.192–94).

So Prospero by his art controls Caliban, who acts as his slave. Caliban acknowledges the overwhelming force of Prospero's magic: "I must obey. His art is of such pow'r / It would control my dam's god, Setebos, / And make a vassal of him" (1.2.374–76). At the beginning of the play, Prospero is in charge of the island and its inhabitants, and his plot to shipwreck Alonso, Sebastian (his brother), and his own brother Antonio when they are coming from the marriage of Alonso's daughter Claribel in Tunis is succeeding perfectly. Ferdinand, Alonso's son, is shipwrecked in another part of the island, where he can fall in love with and marry Miranda, Prospero's daughter. As the master magician says of this love affair, "It works" (1.2.498), but this is also true for his entire elaborate plot.

The last scene of the play begins with Prospero "*in his magic robes*" (5.1.1 s.d.). He says, with some satisfaction: "Now does my project gather to a head. / My charms crack not, my spirits obey, and time / Goes upright with his carriage" (5.1.1–3). His enemies are all in his power. It is at this point that Ariel effects a turn in the action by commenting on the present situation: "Your charm so strongly works 'em, / That if you now beheld them, your affections / Would become tender" (5.1.17–19). "Charm" is a word specifically connected with magic throughout *The Tempest*.

Without much argument, Ariel persuades Prospero to have compassion on his enemies. Ariel, who is only a spirit, declares that his own "affections / Would become tender" "were I human" (5.1.16–17, 20). Prospero agrees, and this is the turning point of the play. From being a heavy father to Miranda (like Capulet is with Juliet in *Romeo and Juliet*) and a commanding master to Caliban and Ariel, Prospero recovers his human warmth and fallibility. He reasons from the way that Ariel, a spirit, feels to his own human emotions that have been suppressed:

Hast thou, which art but air, a touch, a feeling
Of their afflictions, and shall not myself
One of their kind, that relish all as sharply,
Passion as they, be kindlier moved than thou art?
Though with their high wrongs I am struck to th' quick,
Yet with my nobler reason 'gainst my fury
Do I take part. The rarer action is
In virtue than in vengeance. (5.1.21–28)

Like the Duke in *Measure for Measure*, Prospero is resolved to forgive everyone. He also resolves to give up his noble art of magic: "My charms I'll break, their senses I'll restore, / And they shall be themselves" (5.1.31–32).

In the long soliloquy that follows, Prospero reviews examples of his "so potent art" (5.1.50), but he is determined to surrender his omnipotent role of magician:

> But this rough magic
> I here abjure; and when I have required
> Some heavenly music (which even now I do)
> To work mine end upon their senses that
> This airy charm is for, I'll break my staff,
> Bury it certain fathoms in the earth,
> And deeper that did ever plummet sound
> I'll drown my book. (5.1.50–57)

We should note that Prospero engages in forgiveness somewhat hesitantly. To his own brother, Antonio, who has usurped the dukedom of Milan, he seems to offer only a grudging reconciliation:

> For you, most wicked sir, whom to call brother
> Would even infect my mouth, I do forgive
> Thy rankest fault—all of them; and require
> My dukedom of thee, which perforce I know
> Thou must restore. (5.1.130–34)

Antonio doesn't have much choice on what to do, and we never hear him apologizing to the brother he has wronged. This is one of Shakespeare's most memorable insults: "whom to call brother / Would even infect my mouth." Not very forgiving on Prospero's part.

## Chapter Thirty-Three

# The Tragedy of Cardinal Wolsey in *Henry VIII*

The fall of Cardinal Wolsey is presented in terms we have come to expect from Aristotle's *Poetics*. His arrogance and graspingness has made him many enemies, but when he loses power, we tend to sympathize with him in his adversity. Wolsey's tragedy progresses inevitably like a separate action within the play. There is a certain ambiguity about his role. Is he acting primarily as the king's agent, or is he acting on his own behalf? He does the king's bidding to get rid of his wife Katherine, and he does nothing to hinder the king's marriage to Anne Bullen, although he would much prefer someone else. He always acts as the loyal servant of the king.

In the first scene of the play, Wolsey's enemies, the Duke of Buckingham and the Duke of Norfolk, speak strongly against him. Buckingham complains that "No man's pie is freed / From his ambitious finger" (1.1.52–53). But what really irks both dukes is Wolsey's plebeian ancestry: he is spoken of as a butcher's son. Buckingham calls him contemptuously a "keech," a rolled up lump of animal fat, who "can with his very bulk / Take up the rays o' th' beneficial sun" (1.1.55–56)—in other words, win the king's favor (the king symbolized by the sun). It is implied that Wolsey is a "bulky," fat man. Later in the scene, Buckingham makes the same accusation:

> This butcher's cur is venomed-mouthed, and I
> Have not the power to muzzle him. Therefore best
> Not wake him in his slumber. A beggar's book
> Outworths a noble's blood. (1.1.120–23)

Wolsey's learning ("A beggar's book") outclasses ("Outworths") nobility of descent.

There is a certain envy of Wolsey, the commoner, in both of the noble dukes. Norfolk is more specific in his declaiming against the cardinal:

> For, being not propped by ancestry, whose grace
> Chalks successors their way, nor called upon
> For high feats done to th' crown, neither allied
> To eminent assistants, but spiderlike,
> Out of his self-drawing web, 'a gives us note,
> The force of his own merit makes his way—
> A gift that heaven gives for him, which buys
> A place next to the King. (1.1.59–66)

It seems strange that Norfolk should complain that Wolsey has gotten ahead by "The force of his own merit," which is God's gift, and not through noble birth ("ancestry"), nor triumphs in battle ("feats done to th' crown"), nor by powerful friends at court ("eminent assistants"). This seems like pure snobbery on Norfolk's part.

Buckingham cannot abide "This Ipswich fellow's insolence," who seems to "proclaim / There's difference in no persons" (1.1.138–39); in other words, it is insolent to believe that distinctions of noble birth no longer matter. Wolsey is a plebeian upstart. Buckingham cannot contain his vituperation for the cardinal:

> This holy fox,
> Or wolf, or both (for he is equal rav'nous
> As he is subtle, and as prone to mischief
> As able to perform't, his mind and place
> Infecting one another, yea, reciprocally)
> Only to show his pomp as well in France
> As here at home (1.1.158–64)

Before the end of act 1, Buckingham is arrested and sent to the Tower, presumably at Wolsey's behest, and he is shortly to be executed (2.1).

Wolsey is hated by almost everyone in the first acts of the play. In act 1, scene 1, for example, an anonymous Second Gentleman complains: "All the commons / Hate him perniciously, and, o' my conscience, / Wish him ten fathoms deep" (2.1.49–51). In act 2, scene 2, Wolsey is seen as engineering the king's divorce from Katherine. Norfolk calls him "the king-cardinal, / That blind priest, like the eldest son of Fortune, / Turns what he list" (2.2.19–21). All the court fervently wish that the king "will know him one day" (2.2.21). As the Lord Chamberlain says: "Heaven will one day open / The king's eyes, that so long have slept upon / This bold, bad man" (2.2.41–43). So we are ready for this revelation, which will certainly come soon.

At her trial in act 2, scene 4, the queen clearly recognizes Wolsey as her enemy:

> I utterly abhor, yea, from my soul
> Refuse you for my judge, whom, yet once more,
> I hold my most malicious foe, and think not
> At all a friend to truth. (2.4.79–82)

But do we excuse Wolsey as an agent merely acting on the king's behalf, or is he personally responsible for the removal of the queen? The answer to this question remains ambiguous.

Wolsey and Cardinal Campeius visit the queen in act 3, scene 1, presumably to get her consent to the divorce, but Katherine is on to their duplicity: "Ye tell me what ye wish for both—my ruin" (3.1.98). She accuses them of unfeeling, unchristian conduct:

> Holy men I thought ye,
> Upon my soul, two reverend cardinal virtues;
> But cardinal sins and hollow hearts I fear ye.
> Mend 'em, for shame, my lords. (3.1.102–5)

But Wolsey and Campeius seem incapable of feeling much empathy for the suffering queen.

By act 3, scene 2, Wolsey has incurred the displeasure of the king. First of all, Wolsey opposes the king's marriage to Anne Bullen, whom he calls "A spleeny [splenetic] Lutheran, and not wholesome to / Our cause that she should lie i' th' bosom of / Our hard-ruled [hard to advise] king." (3.1.100–102). Then Wolsey is also worried about the sudden rise of Cranmer: "An heretic, an arch one, Cranmer, one / Hath crawled into the favor of the King, / And is his oracle" (3.2.102–4).

But the king has stronger reasons for his disappointment with Wolsey. An inventory of Wolsey's possessions, sent to the king by mistake, signals his downfall. The king is deeply disturbed:

> The several parcels of his plate, his treasure,
> Rich stuffs, and ornaments of household, which
> I find at such proud rate that it outspeaks
> Possession of a subject. (3.2.126–29)

The king understands that Wolsey is not as spiritual as he seems, but, of course, he has always advised the king in secular matters. He reminds the king of "the part of business which / I bear i' th' state" (3.2.146–47), but it is too late, and the king has other ideas in mind. He exits "*frowning upon the Cardinal*" (3.2.203 s.d.).

Right afterward, Wolsey's soliloquy acknowledges his imminent fall, and we begin to commiserate with his fate: "I shall fall / Like a bright exhalation in the evening, / And no man see me more" (3.2.226–28). On the authority of the king, the Duke of Norfolk forces him to surrender the Great Seal, which confirms his high position as lord chancellor.

In another soliloquy he bemoans his downfall in eloquent and sorrowful images:

> I have ventured,
> Like little wanton boys that swim on bladders,
> This many summers in a sea of glory,
> But far beyond my depth. My high-blown pride
> At length broke under me and now has left me,
> Weary and old with service, to the mercy
> Of a rude stream that must forever hide me. (3.2.359–65)

We feel with the cardinal in his adversity, partly because he is so ready to acknowledge his own pride.

He doesn't blame the king but accepts his current situation: "And when he falls, he falls like Lucifer, / Never to hope again" (3.2.372–73). He feels within himself "A peace above all earthly dignities, / A still and quiet conscience. The king has cured me" (3.2.380–81). With a new humility, he releases Cromwell from his service: "I am a poor fall'n man, unworthy now / To be thy lord and master" (3.2.414–15). His final advice to Cromwell sums up his own career: "Had I but served my God with half the zeal / I served my king, he would not in mine age / Have left me naked to mine enemies" (3.2.456–58). Wolsey's words acknowledge that, in his secular commitment to the king, he has neglected his own spiritual role.

We learn about the death of Wolsey in act 4, scene 2, and it is significant that we have two very different character sketches of him by the queen and by Griffith, her Gentleman Usher. Katherine speaks of him as her inveterate enemy:

> He was a man
> Of an unbounded stomach [pride, arrogance], ever ranking
> Himself with princes; one that by suggestion
> Tied all the kingdom. Simony was fair play;
> His own opinion was his law. I' th' presence
> He would say untruths and be ever double
> Both in his words and meaning. He was never,
> But where he meant to ruin, pitiful.
> His promises were, as he then was, mighty,
> But his performance, as he is now, nothing. (4.2.33–42)

Griffith strongly disagrees and presents a contrary portrait of Wolsey's inherent virtues:

> Though from a humble stock, undoubtedly
> Was fashioned to much honor from his cradle.
> He was a scholar, and a ripe and good one;
> Exceeding wise, fair-spoken, and persuading;
> Lofty and sour to them that loved him not,
> But to those men that sought him, sweet as summer.
> And though he were unsatisfied in getting,
> Which was a sin, yet in bestowing, madam,
> He was most princely. (4.2.49–57)

Why does Shakespeare present these two different impressions of Wolsey side by side? I think he wants to be fair to the essential ambiguity of his character. Many of Wolsey's faults come from his devotion to the king, for which he was forced to neglect his spiritual role.

## Chapter Thirty-Four

# The Pretty Madness of the Jailer's Daughter in *The Two Noble Kinsmen*

There is a sharp contrast in this play between the high-born characters in the main plot and the low-born characters in the subplot. The Jailer's Daughter, who is never named (nor is the Jailer, the Wooer, or the Doctor), is a hearty lass, direct and outspoken, who falls in love with Palamon, the nephew of Creon, in the main plot. Otherwise, the two actions never cross. Although the play is probably a collaboration between Shakespeare and John Fletcher, I am treating it without any mention of what may have been Fletcher's share.

The Jailer's Daughter appears in nine scenes and has more lines than Emilia in the main plot. We first see her in act 2, scene 1, where she comments admiringly on the new prisoners, Palamon and Arcite: "the prison itself is proud of 'em" (2.1.26–27), and "It is a holiday to look on them" (2.1.56). By act 2, scene 3, the Jailer's Daughter has already fallen in love with Palamon and expresses her affection in soliloquy:

> Why should I love this gentleman? 'Tis odds
> He never will affect me; I am base,
> My father the mean keeper of his prison,
> And he a prince; to marry him is hopeless,
> To be his whore is witless. Out upon't,
> What pushes are we wenches driven to
> When fifteen once has found us! (2.3.1–7)

Later in the play, the Wooer says she is 18 (5.2.29). It is interesting how many soliloquies she has, which stress her importance in the action. Her soliloquy in act 2, scene 3 is already strongly sexual—"What should I do to make him know I love him, / For I would fain enjoy him? Say I ventured / To

171

set him free?" (2.3.29–31)—which is just what she does without any thought of the consequences for herself and her father. She says she doesn't want to be Palamon's whore, but she wants to enjoy him nevertheless. Marriage is, of course, impossible.

By act 2, scene 5, she has already provided for Palamon's escape and, in another soliloquy, declares her undying love for him. She speaks with romantic intensity:

> O Love,
> What a stout-hearted child thou art! My father
> Durst better have endured cold iron than done it.
> I love him, beyond love and beyond reason,
> Or wit, or safety: I have made him know it.
> I care not, I am desperate. (2.5.8–13)

Remember Imogen's love for Posthumus in *Cymbeline*, which is "beyond beyond" (3.2.56). But the Jailer's Daughter's love is more sexual:

> Let him do
> What he will with me, so he use me kindly,
> For use me so he shall, or I'll proclaim him,
> And to his face, no man. (2.5.28–31)

"No man" means literally that Palamon will be proclaimed impotent.

In another long soliloquy in act 3, scene 2, the Jailer's Daughter is charmingly personal in her grief at not finding Palamon where she left him:

> In me hath grief slain fear, and but for one thing
> I care for nothing, and that's Palamon.
> I reck not if the wolves would jaw me, so
> He had this file. (3.2.5–8)

She is becoming desperate, and there is a fear that she will go mad:

> I am moped:
> Food took I none these two days,
> Sipped some water. I have not closed my eyes
> Save when my lids scoured off their brine. Alas,
> Dissolve my life, let not my sense unsettle,
> Lest I should drown, or stab, or hang myself. (3.2.25–30)

This is the only use of "moped," meaning bewildered, in Shakespeare, and the whole speech expresses not only the Jailer's Daughter's fears but also her innocence. This is the last we see of her before she goes mad in act 3, scene 4. She considers herself a martyr to love.

The presentation of her madness is clearly derived from that of Ophelia in *Hamlet*, but the Jailer's Daughter's madness is more fully developed, and she sings more songs. Both she and Ophelia express a strong sexual innuendo, now that they are freed from the proprieties of civil life. The Jailer's Daughter is lyrical, if not actually pretty, in her expression of wonder at the reality mixed with fantasy that surrounds her. In this she is clearly allied with other heroines of Shakespeare's late romances, like Perdita, Miranda, and Imogen. In another soliloquy in act 3, scene 4, she is still looking for Palamon (as Imogen seeks Posthumus in *Cymbeline*):

> Alas, no, he's in heaven. Where am I now?
> Yonder's the sea, and there's a ship: how't tumbles,
> And there's a rock lies watching under water;
> Now, now, it beats upon it [the ship]; now, now!
> There's a leak sprung, a sound one; how they cry! (3.2.4–8)

This sounds like the shipwreck in *The Tempest*. The Jailer's Daughter is deep into fantasy as she seeks "a fine frog" who "would tell me / News from all parts o' th' world" (3.2.12–13). She ends the scene with a charming, folktale allusion (with strong double entendre): "O for a prick now like a nightingale, / To put my breast against!" (3.2.25–26). To sing, the nightingale was supposed to press against a thorn to stay awake. In the next scene, she participates, as "a dainty mad woman" (3.5.73), in the interlude that the Schoolmaster is putting on for the court. Her speech is still interlarded with covert sexual allusions: "I know you, y' are a tinker: sirrah tinker, / Stop no more holes but what you should" (3.2.83–84).

By act 4, scene 3, the Doctor has appeared to counsel her father and the Wooer. He resembles the doctor in *Macbeth*, who asserts about the mad Lady Macbeth: "More needs she the divine than the physician" (5.1.78). In *The Two Noble Kinsmen*, however, the Doctor empathizes with the Jailer's Daughter: "How prettily she's amiss!" and "How her brain coins!" (4.3.28, 39), but he also has a credible diagnosis: "'Tis not an engraffed madness, but a most thick and profound melancholy" (4.3.47–49). Although he confesses that she has "a perturbed mind, which I cannot minister to" (4.3.58–59), he does have a practical, sexual solution: the Wooer should pretend that he is Palamon, woo the Jailer's Daughter, promise her marriage, and, eventually, sleep with her. Shakespeare devotes careful attention to the Doctor's psychological cure: "It is a falsehood she is in, which is with falsehoods to be combated. This may bring her to eat, to sleep, and reduce what's now out of square in her into their former law and regiment" (4.3.93–95). The Doctor knows from experience that the sexual cure will work.

The Doctor continues his role as therapist in act 5, scene 2, where he has practical sexual advice for the Wooer, who is now dressed in Palamon's clothes. It is all summed up in "And when your fit comes, fit her home, and presently" (5.2.11)—in other words, lie with her and be vigorous about it. The Wooer seems to need encouragement, so that the Doctor is forced to become more and more explicit: "Please her appetite / And do it home: it cures her *ipso facto* / The melancholy humor that infects her" (5.2.35–37). After a number of lyrical exchanges, the Jailer's Daughter seems to be on the way to recovering her sanity. But, of course, it all depends on the love and sexual participation of the Wooer, who still plays the role of Palamon. The scene ends on an upbeat of romantic harmony:

*Daughter.* And then we'll sleep together?

*Doctor.* Take her offer.

*Wooer.* Yes, marry will we.

*Daughter.* But you shall not hurt me.

*Wooer.* I will not, sweet.

*Daughter.* If you do, love, I'll cry. (5.2.109–11)

It is an appropriately lyrical end for the eminently sweet and innocent Jailer's Daughter.

# Conclusion

The main observation one can make about Shakespeare's style is that it is different in different plays. Nonetheless, there are patterns in Shakespeare's art. For one, while nearly all of his plays derive from earlier sources, Shakespeare always succeeds not just in appropriating their stories but in making them his own. *The Comedy of Errors*, for example, is based on Plautus, the prolific Roman writer of comedies of the third and second century BCE, but Shakespeare goes Plautus one better by doubling the number of servants and masters. *Love's Labor's Lost*, in its elaborate and fanciful style, owes a great debt to John Lyly, an English writer who was a contemporary of Shakespeare's. Romantic comedies like *The Two Gentlemen of Verona, Twelfth Night*, and *As You Like It* rely on the romantic conventions set forth in the primarily Italian and Spanish stories Shakespeare read. His English history plays owe much of their factual material to Raphael Holinshed's *Chronicles* (1577), and Sir Thomas North's translation of Plutarch's *Lives* (1579) provides Shakespeare with important insights about character that he uses in his Roman plays, especially *Julius Caesar* and *Antony and Cleopatra*. The important point is that Shakespeare is never content simply to repeat his source.

There are certain kinds of characters that seem to appeal to Shakespeare. I am thinking particularly of the long line of Shakespeare's villains. Aaron in *Titus Andronicus* serves as a kind of template for the many villains that follow. He is a laughing, sardonic villain, like the Vice figure in medieval plays, and the villains that come after him—like Richard, Duke of Gloucester in *3 Henry VI* and *Richard III*, Iago in *Othello*, and Edmund in *King Lear*—are all like him in many ways. They are all witty, histrionic figures who make important use of slang and colloquial speech.

Another group of characters special to Shakespeare are satirical observers, often playing the role of calumniators. Lucio in *Measure for Measure* is a good example. Without any personal motivation, he freely slanders the absent duke, but, in the course of his vituperation, he is also a truth speaker who has keen insights into the duke's limitations. Similarly, Apemantus in *Timon of Athens* comments on the extravagances of Timon, and the scurrilous Thersites in *Troilus and Cressida* presents the anti-heroic side of the Trojan War. Perhaps the melancholy Jaques in *As You Like It* also belongs in this group. He entertains the exiled court of Duke Senior with his sour view of the world, especially in his speech on the seven ages of man.

One is impressed with the self-consciousness of Shakespeare's characters, especially those who communicate directly with the audience through soliloquies and asides. This is especially true of a character like Hamlet, who, in his several soliloquies, shows us what he is thinking in contrast to what is going on in the stage action. He is also critical of his own ranting style, for example, when he jumps into Ophelia's grave with Laertes. Shakespeare's characters—especially his villains—are great soliloquizers because they are anxious that the audience know exactly what they are thinking. The many soliloquies in *Macbeth* keep us aware of Macbeth's acute sense of guilt, which tends to become an apathetic despair in the latter part of the play. King Lear, too, in his soliloquies and his oncoming madness, changes in his perception of the world (with its poor naked wretches) and of the true nature of his daughters. Although she is not a thoughtful, meditative character like Hamlet, the Jailer's Daughter in *The Two Noble Kinsmen* repeatedly expresses herself in soliloquy. We find soliloquies in unexpected places in Shakespeare, and at times they have a strictly expository function.

In a more limited, rhetorical sense of style, Shakespeare has a wide range of ways he can speak to us. For example, he uses varied (sometimes unanticipated) imagery and symbolism to present his meanings. We are not prepared for the repetition of skin images in *Hamlet*, especially images of a hidden and inner pathology to convey the sense of poisonous secrecy in the play. In *Troilus and Cressida*, food and eating images suggest the folly and disgust of the Trojan War, especially in its erotic dimension. There is no possibility of true love here—only lust. This resembles Iago's view of Desdemona (and all women) in *Othello*. Villains like Iago and Aaron are skillful masters of slang and colloquial language in their plays. Sexuality, which is either overtly or covertly (in double entendres and innuendo) present in all of Shakespeare, is the theme of much wordplay in the comedies, especially by clowns, fools, and lower-class characters. These characters are often illiterate and speak English not as it is written but phonetically, as does the Nurse in *Romeo and Juliet* and Dame Quickly in the *Henry IV* plays and *The Merry Wives of Windsor*. As an aspect of Shakespeare's art, we should also note how the blank verse in the late romances (*Pericles, Cymbeline, The Winter's Tale,* and *The Tempest*) breaks the expected iambic pentameter pattern and tries to follow speech rhythms.